HAUNTINGS
⊰ OF THE ⊱
UNDERGROUND
RAILROAD

HAUNTINGS
⊰ OF THE ⊱
UNDERGROUND
RAILROAD

Ghosts of the Midwest

JANE SIMON AMMESON

INDIANA UNIVERSITY PRESS

This book is a publication of

Indiana University Press
Office of Scholarly Publishing
Herman B Wells Library 350
1320 East 10th Street
Bloomington, Indiana 47405 USA

iupress.indiana.edu

The paper used in this publication meets the minimum requirements of
the American National Standard for Information Sciences—Permanence
of Paper for Printed Library Materials, ANSI Z39.48-1992.

Manufactured in the United States of America

Cataloging information is available from the Library of Congress.

ISBN 978-0-253-03128-0 (cloth)
ISBN 978-0-253-02982-9 (paperback)
ISBN 978-0-253-03129-7 (ebook)

1   2   3   4   5   22   21   20   19   18   17

CONTENTS

PREFACE
vii

1   Phantom of the Cellar
1

2   Spirits of the Waters
19

3   Sold down the River:
The Reverse Underground Railroad
41

4   Lincoln Walks at Midnight
50

5   Outwitting the Devil
63

6   Ghostly Overload
81

7   A Room with a Ghoul
101

8   John Hunt Morgan
108

9   The Last Trip Home
123

10   Michigan's Haunted Underground Railroad
147

11   The Conductor and the Slave:
The Story of Levi Coffin and William Bush
162

12   Restless Spirits
171

13   There Should Be Ghosts!
176

SELECTED BIBLIOGRAPHY
185

PREFACE

A COLD DAMP fog descends as the whistle of a steam locomotive sounds off in the distance. Clocks and watches stop, making time stand still as the nine-car Lincoln Special emerges into sight. This isn't the original Lincoln funeral train that left Washington, D.C., on April 21, 1865, carrying the bodies of the 16th president and his 11-year-old son on a 1,654-mile journey, the reverse of the one Lincoln had taken from Springfield, Illinois, to Washington, D.C., in celebration of his election just four years earlier.

Instead, it's a ghost train, following the same schedule, arriving at each stop on the same day and time as on Lincoln's final journey. Want to see the Lincoln Special go by? Pick a former stop, preferably one where modern civilization seems far away, and wait. Funeral music and metal wheels on metal rails announce the arrival of the truly skeletal crew manning the engine house and stoking the fires as phantom Union soldiers continue, as they have for more than 150 years, to stand sentry over the coffin of their fallen president.

Just north of Indianapolis, in Westfield, a Union soldier walks the perimeter of the Anti-Slavery Friends Cemetery, stopping at a gravesite—that of a soldier slain in the last days

President Abraham Lincoln's hearse in Springfield, Illinois. On April 21, 1865, Lincoln's funeral train left Washington, D.C., on its 1,654-mile journey, traveling through 180 cities and 7 states, to Springfield, Illinois, where Lincoln would be buried on May 4. But the president's burial wouldn't end the funeral train's travel. Each year the train, its mournful whistle sounding, journeys again along the same route, the casket still guarded by ghostly Union soldiers. Photo courtesy of the Library of Congress.

of the war. Whose grave is he guarding? Is it that of a comrade gone too soon in battle? Or is it his own?

Before the Civil War, the Great Lake states had many trails to freedom for African Americans escaping slavery. It was a perilous journey, as slave hunters offering large bounties for the return of "property" pursued them, and laws made those who helped slaves subject to harsh fines, loss of property, and even imprisonment. But freedom overrode all concerns and slaves ran away, crossing into Indiana, Illinois, Ohio, Michigan, and Wisconsin on to Canada, where slavery

One of the most haunted Civil War cemeteries, the Confederate Stockade Cemetery is located on the three-hundred-acre Johnson's Island in Lake Erie, near Sandusky, Ohio. A prison that housed approximately fifteen thousand Confederate soldiers was on Johnson's Island. The ghosts of many, including the two hundred buried there, engage in phantom battles and march along with the living during Memorial Day parades. Photo courtesy of the Library of Congress.

was illegal; these concerns also didn't stop those helpers who believed in a higher cause than manmade laws—be it attributed to a higher being or their own conscience and sense of justice.

In 1831, Tice Davids, a slave from Maysville, Kentucky, swam across the Ohio River to the free state of Ohio. His owner, following closely behind in a skiff, came ashore shortly after Davids did. But the slave had already disappeared and all those whom the slave owner questioned denied having seen Davids.

"He must have gone on some underground road," the slave master said, and thus the Underground Railroad, or, for

Though they look like the ghostly remains of stunted trees, these structures are really chimneys for the rathskeller at McCourtie Park in Somerset, Michigan, a stop on the Underground Railroad. Photo courtesy of Jane Simon Ammeson.

short, UGRR, came to mean the complex spiderlike system of trails African Americans followed as they made their way north.

Stationmasters oversaw the "depots" which were homes and businesses offering shelter, a place to rest and eat; stockholders contributed money and goods; and the conductors helped fugitives move from one station to the next.

Together these people were the counterforce to slave owners and the institution of slavery—men and women not interested in money but in justice. And what they achieved is legendary.

With two children dead and buried, the thought of her last remaining child being sold into slavery made Eliza Harris determined, no matter the danger, to make her way from Kentucky to Canada and freedom. And so, late one night, Harris bundled up her two-year-old daughter and crossed the winter landscape to the shores of the Ohio River.

Her plan was to walk across the frozen waters, but a thaw had turned the solid ice into chunks. When the weather didn't change and with her pursuers getting closer, Harris

The former home of Nathaniel Hanson, owner of Alton Machine Shop & Foundry and a fierce abolitionist, has passageways and rooms fifteen feet below street level, providing shelter for runaways. The building later became the Enos Sanitarium, and now, crowded with ghosts, it is the Enos Apartments, often included on tours of Haunted Alton. Photo courtesy of Alton Regional Convention and Visitors Bureau.

took the risk, wading into the freezing water, climbing on and off ice floes drifting along the wide river until she miraculously found her way to Indiana soil.

Harris's journey was far from over. Because of the success of the Underground Railroad, the Fugitive Acts were broadened in 1850, and anyone assisting or helping hide fugitive slaves could be sent to prison and fined $1,000—almost $50,000 in today's currency. Slave hunters also were allowed to come north into free states and capture runaways; it was bounty hunting with huge financial rewards.

Luckily, Harris had come ashore in just the right spot— not far from the home of Quaker Levi Coffin, a successful merchant who had earned the nickname "president of the Underground Railroad."

Levi and Catharine Coffin, who lived in southeastern Indiana, believed so fervently in the antislavery movement that they helped an estimated two thousand slaves escape. Now their home—a two-story, eight-room red-brick house built in 1839 in Fountain City near Richmond—is a national historic landmark and was named one of the top twenty-five historic sites by the History Channel.

From this house, Harris and her daughter made their way to Canada, where they prospered. Years later, she would see the Coffins, who were visiting Ontario, and thank them for all that they had done. Harris's ordeal was immortalized when Harriet Beecher Stowe, a staunch abolitionist, retold her story in her novel *Uncle Tom's Cabin*, keeping the name the same. Thus, the world learned the horrors of slavery and Harris's bravery.

Slave hunters were not only greedy and cruel but cunning as well. Violent men, they used violence to achieve their means, and so Underground Railroad conductors like Levi Coffin had to be even more cunning. Tricks of the trade for Coffin and other conductors included false-bottomed carriages, wagons with boxes for concealment, hidden rooms, underground tunnels, and signals used to let others know when there was danger and when it was safe to move. Coffin, well versed in the law, also used his legal knowledge to defeat slave owners in court. Along with many others, he used his own money to help runaways gain freedom.

"The Underground Railroad business increased as time advanced and it was attended with heavy expenses which I could not have borne had not my affairs been prosperous," he wrote in his 1876 book *Reminiscences of Levi Coffin*.

But for all those like the Coffins, willing to risk everything, there were others in free states whose sympathies were definitely Southern. Some even ran a reverse UGRR where free blacks were kidnapped and forced into slavery with the use of falsified papers and owners deep in the South who did not care about such technicalities as whether a man was free or not. Slavery was even legal in Illinois for certain reasons. Though it was a free state, representatives, pandering to wealthy men who had salt mine leases and complained about not finding enough free men willing to work (most likely because they didn't want to pay them fair wages for the grueling labor), made it legal for them to own slaves.

Running away into what was in many ways the unknown, slaves were vulnerable to disease, starvation, weather extremes, and other dangerous situations where something could, and frequently did, go very wrong indeed.

Thus the sounds of slaves dying in a fire at an Underground Railroad station, in what is now a historic bed-and-breakfast in Indianapolis, and the roaming ghost of a Union soldier killed in battle and buried in a mass grave, whose body was retrieved by his wealthy father and brought back home, are among many of the stories of hauntings along the Underground Railroad in the Great Lakes states.

Though I'm not a historian by training, I come from a family of history buffs who can dig down into the minutiae with an amazing passion. Ask my brother how many electoral votes presidential candidate Alf Landon got, and he'll tell you and also name the states Landon won, while my father could recount which West Point class produced the most soldiers who first fought together in Mexico during the Mexican-American War and then on opposite sides during the War between the States.

In keeping as much historic accuracy as possible, I tried to take each of the stories in this book and trace its roots, sorting out, as best as I could, myth from reality—or as much reality as you can find on the Underground Railroad, where, because of its very nature, nothing much was recorded. And as far as ghost stories go, they are folkloric rather than hard history and thus undocumented, except in oral history and tradition.

But I tried my best, talking to historical societies, librarians, innkeepers, preservationists, restaurant owners, museum docents, paranormal investigators, authors of ghost books and tomes about the Underground Railroad, and anyone I could get in touch with who owned or was associated with a building or site said to be haunted by ghosts of the UGRR. I had the honor to meet Eileen Baker-Wall, whose great-great-grandfather, William Bush, was a runaway slave who found shelter at the home of Levi Coffin, maybe the greatest conductor on the Underground Railroad ever. Bush then went on to settle in Fountain City, Indiana, open a blacksmith shop, and become a conductor himself. I combed the digitalized archives—I subscribe to three, the *New York Times* Time-Machine, newspapers.com, and newspaperarchives.com, and also almost obsessively browsed Chronicling America, which is available for free through the Library of Congress and which has an amazing collection of periodicals from 1789 to 1924, and another free resource, Hoosier State Chronicles, a digitalized collection of newspapers throughout Indiana.

Of course I've learned so much: how funeral practices were conducted back in the 1800s; how people lived and died (at least two of the people in my chapters died in horse-related accidents); and how many of these stories got reported by German newspapers—most likely because there was such a huge influx of German immigrants to the Midwest.

By talking to paranormal investigators such as Mary Barrett of Paranormal 911, I've learned about ghost hunting, including the delicate communication between the living and dead and the equipment needed for a thorough investigation.

Why are some places haunted and others, with just as many reasons to host a ghost or two, not? I asked Barrett about the *SS Argosy*, a steamer that exploded on the Ohio River as it carried Union soldiers returning home at the end of the Civil War. Twelve men died and are buried in a mass grave on the Ohio. Why wasn't that place haunted?

Her reply was informative and helped me understand how hauntings—and thus stories—come to be.

"It could be haunted but maybe it's such a lost piece of history that most ghost hunters haven't heard about it yet." Mary told me about the speck of a town once named Rono, after the postmaster's much beloved dog, and later changed to Magnet. "Nearly every place holds at least some residual energy. Though not all places have intelligent spirits. Our team might take a road trip down there to see what we can find."

I hope she goes soon as I'd like to be a part of a newly discovered haunting.

Oh, and what, you may ask, are intelligent spirits? Barrett explained this to me as well. It's the type of haunting where the spiritual entity is aware of its surroundings and able to communicate in some way. They're typically not malevolent but instead are like most of us. All they want is some appreciation and respect.

Indeed, stories of malicious hauntings were rare in the stories I gathered. A few chased people, gave a push or two, and were generally unpleasant. But for the most part, it was interesting how quickly ghosts adapted to the people around them, seen here and there and just as quickly gone.

Now it comes to thanking people, and I am so anxious I left someone out from this very long list. If I did, I am so terribly sorry. It was more about making my deadline than not realizing how important you were to all this.

Thanks to Ashley Runyon and Peggy Solic, my editors at Indiana University Press, for making this book possible. A big shout-out to Kathy Neff, my editor at *AAA Magazine* Hoosier Edition, who gave me my first assignment to write about the Underground Railroad, which opened up this amazing history to me, and to Nancy Sartain, leisure marketing director, Richmond-Wayne County Convention & Tourism Bureau, who introduced me to the UGRR in her part of the state, including the Levi Coffin home.

Others who gave me invaluable assistance are (in no particular order):

Marty Bacon, manager, Slippery Noodle Inn, Indianapolis, Indiana.

Eileen Baker-Wall, great-great-granddaughter of William Bush and volunteer at the Levi Coffin State Historic Site and Interpretative Center.

Tony Barger, Putnam County Public Library.

Barbara Bradley, owner, National House, Marshall, Indiana.

Jeffrey Cole, trustee, G. W. Adams Educational Center.

Tony Collignon, Perry County historian and president of the Perry County Historical Society.

Susan Collins, my coauthor for the book *Marshall, Indiana*.

Helen Einhaus, Ripley County, Indiana, historian.

Tom and Melody Fucik, owners, Millstone of Iola Mill, Iola, Wisconsin.

Fred Griffin, who, before he died, shared stories his grandmother had told him about Morgan's raid.

Cathy Hoben, whom I met on Isla de Ixtapa and talked to about the Underground Railroad stories she remembered from growing up in Adrian, Michigan.

John Johnson, M.D., owner, Inn at Aberdeen.

Mike Kienzler, historian and researcher, Sangamon County Historical Society.

Michael and Nicole Kobrowski, authors, owners of Indiana Ghost Walks and Tours.

John Koch, member of McCourtie Park, Somerset, Michigan.

Eva Lindsay, Genealogy Department, Spencer County
   Public Library.
Scott Lonuerer, owner, Hannah House, Indianapolis,
   Indiana.
Betty Manning, whose family owns Stream Cliff Farms
   and who showed me the fireplace where John Hunt
   Morgan found the hidden treasures of the home's first
   owner.
Mark Marimen, author of several books about Indiana
   hauntings.
Janice McGuire, volunteer for forty years at the Levi Coffin
   State Historic Site and Interpretative Center.
Brad Mikulka, leader of the Lansing-based SouthEast
   Michigan Ghost Hunters Society.
Melanie Miller, resident of Rockport, Indiana, who owns an
   1840 home that was part of the Underground Railroad,
   though we don't know if it's haunted or not.
William T. Miller, Southern Indiana Paranormal
   Investigators.
Lisa Harris Mock, executive director, Putnam County
   Museum.
Garret Moffett, Lincoln's Ghost Walk, Springfield, Illinois.
Craig Nehring, founder, Fox Valley Ghost Hunters.
Becky Nelson, Alton Visitors Bureau.
Diane Coon Perrine, historian.
Megan Renfro, Putnam County Museum.
Stacey Schulte, owner, Rockport Inn.
Linda Simon, my coauthor for the book *Miller Beach*.
Ruth Slottag, president, Sangamon County Historical
   Society, Illinois.
Troy Taylor, author.
Larry Tiffin, Putnam County historian.
Wanda Willis, author, whom I interviewed before her
   death.

Hal Yeagy, owner, Slippery Noodle Inn, Indianapolis,
   Indiana.
And my children, Evan and Nia Ammeson, whom I love
   more than anything.

HAUNTINGS
OF THE
UNDERGROUND
RAILROAD

ONE

Phantom of the Cellar

SLIPPERY NOODLE INN
INDIANAPOLIS, INDIANA

A type of ghostly meet-and-greet place, the Slippery Noodle Inn on South Meridian Street in Indianapolis has attracted an assortment of spirit residents for more than 170 years. It's a former stop on the Underground Railroad, and at least one of those haunting the place is a runaway slave.

"We've got a lot of ghosts," says owner Hal Yeagy. "That's because a lot has happened here since the place opened."

Indeed, this is the oldest bar in the state, and there seems to be no end to the phantom-producing incidents, which Yeagy is more than happy to list.

"In 1912, one of the customers got into a fight with another customer over a girl and stabbed him, leaving the bloody knife on the bar," says Yeagy, whose parents bought the business in 1963 when he was about six. "Of course, when the police came, no one had seen a thing."

Add to that the suicide in the basement of a former owner, the death of a three-year-old who was playing with matches and caught on fire, and a customer who, after shooting another man, said in wonderment, "I don't know why I

In its more than 160 years in business, the Slippery Noodle Inn, a stop on the Underground Railroad, has attracted its share of ghosts, including George, a relic from the Underground Railroad days who stays in the basement. Photo courtesy of Hal Yeagy.

did that." During Prohibition, both the Brady and the Dillinger gangs used what had been a livery in the back of the saloon for target practice. Pigs and cattle were slaughtered in the basement (you can still see the meat hooks used to hang the carcasses), and liquor was distilled and beer brewed down there as well.

And while we're not saying he's haunting the place, back in the day, James Whitcomb Riley tipped more than a few drinks in the bar—not an atypical occurrence for the famed Hoosier poet.

"There was a pumpkin patch between here and the train station just up the street and supposedly Riley, after drinking too much at the bar, fell asleep on his way home right in front of the pumpkins," says general manager Marty Bacon, who has worked at the Slippery Noodle for a quarter of a century. "When he awoke amongst the pumpkins, he felt inspired and wrote his famous poem 'When the Frost Is on the Punkin.'"

Ah . . . poetic inspiration comes from many sources.

Through the decades, staff at the Slippery Noodle Inn have learned to get along with the spirits, some of whom have been there longer than anyone else. Photo courtesy of Hal Yeagy.

Yeagy isn't sure how old the building is—Indianapolis title records from 1920 and before were mostly destroyed when the city flooded, he says—but he's been able to trace it back to 1850 when it was the Tremont House.

"They were trying to be fancy with the name," he says, noting that it was a railroad hotel offering guests food, drink, and a place to stay.

Over the years, its name changed more than once. In the 1860s it became the Concordia House, named after the *Concord*, the first German Lutheran immigrant ship to land in the United States. The next name—the Germania House—continued to reflect the heritage both of the owners and of the patrons in this predominantly German section of Indianapolis. But when World War I started and being German wasn't necessarily cool, the owner, whose last name was Beck, dropped Germania and changed the name to Beck's Saloon. Before Prohibition, Walter Moore bought the business.

"It became Moore's Saloon until Prohibition, so then they called it Moore's Restaurant but you could still drink, and then Prohibition ended and it was called Moore's Saloon again," says Yeagy.

Whatever the name, for a long time it functioned as a hotel as well as an eatery.

Guests slept in the small rooms off the long hallway on the second floor, where at the end there was a communal bathroom with an old claw-foot tub. We're not sure who was in charge of cleaning that tub; it's a subject we don't want to think about too much. By the mid-twentieth century some of these rooms were no longer used for sleeping but for working gals entertaining gentlemen in exchange for cash.

While UGRR sites are typically undocumented, the building itself yields clues as to its history as a stop on the Underground Railroad, says Yeagy.

"The basement floor was dug down deeper than it needed to be," he says. "And there are all sorts of little rooms that you kind of have to half bend over to get into."

There is even more proof. When Yeagy's parents, Harold and Lorean, were still running the place, a family came in. They had an ancestor who was a fugitive slave and they wanted to see what the inn looked like.

"They said their relative had stayed here because it was a part of the Underground Railroad and they had these bits of a diary he'd written talking about it," says Yeagy. "It makes sense. Indiana was a free state and at the time we were located on the southern end of the city, which would be a good location. And near the railroad station, there were always a lot of people coming and going."

Though Yeagy has never actually seen an apparition, he's had lots of strange experiences at the Slippery Noodle.

"When I took over in 1984 the place was literally just the front bar room where we had five or six bright orange booths and ice cream parlor stools," he says. "The place was a mess. The ceiling upstairs was falling in. I was the only one working there and I still had my other job. I had people help and I was remodeling the back room. My girlfriend Carol at the time, now my wife, would help me. I had everything padlocked up, there were steel gates, which I would close. When we got back in the morning, the steel gates would be open and the two-by-fours I was using would be stacked up. It was scary the first few times but then I figured, what the heck."

Yeagy's felt the cold spots. When he's working late at night in his office on the second floor, the only person in the buildings, he hears footsteps, doors closing, and someone calling his name. The ghosts also have some tech skills—all the music on Yeagy's computer was deleted.

"We had everything backed up but still," says Yeagy. "A lot of things get moved around. But most of what I experience is just the overall feel of the place. I talk to the ghosts all the time."

When Yeagy's son Brian began posting about ghostly incidents on the Slippery Noodle's Twitter feed, the ghostly happenings increased to the point that Yeagy decided to delete the tweets.

"We were just getting too much activity," he says. "It was just getting them too riled up."

One time, things got a little strange—more than the usual activity and cold spots and things going bump in the night. No one knew exactly what was going on until they got a call from Carol Yeagy's sister. She's an empath, someone so in tune to other's feeling that it's painful for her to go out of the house.

"She called us up," Yeagy says about his sister-in-law, "and told us that a new ghost had moved in and he's scaring the other ghosts. She says I'll get him out, and within a few days, it was like a black veil being lifted or a dark cloud being blown away. Bad things stopped happening and the employees were happier."

As for Marty Bacon, well, he says he's been around so long (he started as a bouncer in 1991), he thinks the ghosts have come to know him. He says he talks to them sometimes and also leaves a shot of whiskey on the bar in case one of the spooks is thirsty. He's heard doors slamming and footsteps on the floorboards even when he was the only one in the building. Voices call his name, sometimes in a very demanding way.

The first time he was alone and something unusual happened, Bacon thought someone had hidden in the restaurant until everyone had left. So he searched, but no one was there. For the most part he's okay with the ghosts, but there's one he calls the shadow man, a shadowy apparition who "creeps him out."

"Our big music room used to be the stable where people would keep their horses when they'd come in to get a drink or spend the night. Upstairs was the hayloft which are now offices and storage," says Bacon. "One time I was leading a psychic and twenty people around and the psychic says there's the Boss and I'm one of his employees.

"He owned the stable and keeps his lockbox up here—he's a heavyset white guy with a pitted face," says Bacon, recalling the description the psychic gave them.

Turns out that "the Boss" didn't like Bacon—maybe he resented another "boss" being around.

"The psychics—this one was from New Orleans—said the other spirits respected me except for the one guy, the Boss, and she said he bumps into you."

"It gave me cold goosebumps," says Bacon. "My grandmother used to say when that happened it was like someone had stepped on your grave."

The Boss needed a little help but was finally convinced to move on. But as one ghost leaves, more come, says Bacon.

"According to the psychic from New Orleans, we've been around so long, we've become like a spirit magnet," he says. "When they tear down one of the old houses around here, then the spirits come here because they're comfortable here and because we're old."

Though most of the people who work at the inn who've experienced the ghostly ambience say the basement is the most haunted, Bacon finds that most of his experiences happen on the main floor in the back bar area or upstairs in the office. There's Sara, the apparition dressed in a long blue turn-of-the-last-century dress who is sad because one of her customers killed her. How do they know her name? Several staff members took an Ouija board to where the Lady in Blue hangs out—often upstairs where the hotel rooms were or on a balcony overlooking the stage. The planchette spelled out her name. The lady in blue was the madam of the bordello and she's angry because the place isn't the same anymore.

One employee heard pounding footsteps coming after him in the basement and started running for the stairs. The footsteps got louder and faster behind him, but once he got upstairs he was okay. The whole experience left him shaken. But, mostly, the ghosts are just part of the team working at the Noodle.

Bacon thinks he's figured out which ghost hails back to the Underground Railroad.

"It's probably George," he says. "George is an older black man in denim overalls and is down in the basement. One of the psychics says that he did odd jobs and helped people who were on the Underground Railroad get out."

George is a friendly spirit and doesn't bother anyone. Whether he's helping the same UGRR travelers as he did back then, Yeagy and Bacon don't know. He's just there. One of their beer distributors ran into George in the narrow hallway of the basement and when he went upstairs and asked about the other man, he was told there was no one down there but him.

"He refuses to come back and all the guys he works with make fun of him," says Bacon.

A woman making deliveries also ran into George and she nodded at him and he nodded back. She found out later he was a ghost.

But George, Sara, and the other spirits don't bother Yeagy or Bacon. As for the other ghosts, now that the Boss and the spirit who was scaring the other spirits are gone, the two men are rather philosophical about the remaining spooks.

"I figure they're a lot better than some customers," says Bacon. "A ghost isn't going to drink my booze or take my money."

BONAPARTE'S RETREAT
NAPOLEON, INDIANA

Southeastern Indiana, with its scenic panoramas of the Ohio River, hillsides dotted with farms, and nineteenth-century towns, is a beautiful slice of Hoosier homeland, a seemingly placid and gentle place. But back in the mid-1800s, there were invisible trails through this pastoral prettiness, and it's estimated that there were some three hundred sites in southeastern Indiana where people hid or helped runaway slaves. Because the Underground Railroad was a secret organization that survived only by stealth, much of the history of those who helped, those who traveled its routes, and even where they stayed has been lost. But there are still remnants—a home here, a historic marker there—that tell the story.

Once known as the Railroad Inn, Bonaparte's Retreat in Napoleon, Indiana, was a stop on the Underground Railroad. Charlie, the ghost who lives in the basement, was a runaway slave who continued to help others make their way to freedom. Photo courtesy of Kendal Miller.

The Central House in Napoleon, Indiana, is said to be haunted by Underground Railroad ghosts. Photo courtesy of Kendal Miller.

And sometimes there's even more than that. In the small hamlet of Napoleon, William Love and William Howe bought a brick tavern in 1852. Like many new owners, they modified the 1832 building's design, adding a few special touches for their ultimate goal—becoming a station on the UGRR as it coursed through Ripley County.

Love renamed the tavern the Railroad House Hotel, a dig at slave seekers. The only railroad in the small town was the underground one. And even after all these years, both the physical and astral aspects of that time remain.

"There's a dead space between two walls and then a hidden room and tunnel on the south side of the building that no one knew about," says former county historian Helen Einhaus about what is now a busy restaurant called Bonaparte's Retreat.

The room was only accessible by the trap door from inside the tavern—a drop of ten feet and a tunnel leading out to a millpond.

"Unfortunately, though the tunnel and room are still there, the building is now a restaurant," continues Einhaus, who created, with historian Diane Perrine Coon, the five driving tours in Ripley County that follow the main routes of the UGGR. "The owners can't let people in the basement."

But while visitors of the here and now can't frequent the basement, there are others who do so quite regularly and who also make their way through other floors of the building.

"There's the Lady in White, who only haunts the kitchen," says Kayla Reynolds, who with her husband, Ron, owns Bonaparte's Retreat. "Ghosts like kitchens and they also like steps, and my steps go straight down from the upstairs to the kitchen."

If Reynolds seems somewhat blasé about the woman wearing white, it's because she's spent so much time with her since the couple purchased the restaurant. Harmless, this ghost comes and goes as she pleases, and staff there, even if at first they're startled and uneasy, get comfortable with her presence.

Mary Barrett's father grew up in Napoleon, and she still has relatives living there.

"Some of my cousins were telling me about paranormal activity in town and at Bonaparte's," says Barrett, cofounder, with her husband, Sean, of Paranormal 911 Investigations, LLC.

About five years ago, Barrett talked to the then-owners, who okayed her team coming in and conducting an investigation.

"That first night, we concentrated primarily on the double dug basement," says Barrett, who shared a video of what looked like a long night of waiting for ghostly happenings. "The tunnel's entrance is boarded up and so you can't access it. But it was the place where there would have been the most activity, which is why we stayed nearby."

Ghost hunting requires a lot of scientific-sounding equipment, and Barrett explains what type of data they were able to collect during their first investigation at Bonaparte's. Their EMF meter, an instrument measuring the fluctuation in electromagnetic fields, was able to pick up voices, odd noises, and strange sounds. While staking out the dark basement ("lights out" is a prerequisite when looking for ghosts), they felt the rush of ice cold breezes coming from—well, nowhere. As quickly as the drafts blew in, they'd disappear again. Spirits have personalities, and one of the ghosts on the scene was rather feisty, developing a yen for a female paranormal investigator. But later research determined he wasn't from the UGRR days.

Back when the tunnel was accessible, it was part of a triad of buildings, including a livery that was just across the street and the Conwell House located about a block away.

"Local historians report that slaves were transported in a false-bottom wagon hauling a pig," says Barrett. "The pig was so used to the routine that it would automatically walk up into the wagon and wait for it to be loaded."

According to Barrett, the tunnel was built on a diagonal to the livery. When the wagon arrived, the driver would pull it inside the livery and the slaves would get out, descend into the tunnel, and walk under the road to the inn's basement, where they hid until it was time to take the next leg of their journey.

That, most likely, is how Charlie got into the basement at Bonaparte's Retreat.

"One of the bartenders at Bonaparte's had repeatedly described seeing a black man at the bottom of the stairway," says Barrett about Charlie, a black man wearing bib overalls. Thought to be a runaway slave, he stays in the basement, frequently in the secret room, and other areas. No one is sure why he is still there, instead of continuing on with the other slaves, but Barrett has a theory.

"We feel that Charlie's role when he was alive was to help others get to their next destination, but he didn't go himself as he's still around," says Barrett, noting that the TV show *My Ghost Story* filmed a segment on their Bonaparte's Retreat investigation, which is available on the show's website. "We don't really know for certain if any of the male voices captured down there are his or not. That's because there are a lot of different voices—men, women, and children. For some reason Charlie is still here as if he's protecting other slaves and helping them. When you stand by the tunnel entrance, you periodically feel a rush of air pass by and the meters light up. We decided that was when they'd open the tunnel doors so people could get in or out."

Interestingly, though there are many spirits roaming the entire building, most of those connected to the UGRR seem to haunt only the basement.

Besides doing their own investigations, Paranormal 911 often lent their equipment to others during the public ghost hunts they held. During these hunts, guests worked along-side them.

"Other ghosts made their presence known at the inn during these times," says Barrett.

Ghosts from different eras and life situations seem to intermingle down in the basement, and while many were escaped slaves traveling north, others, such as the flirty gent, weren't part of the Underground Railroad but had other associations with the building.

Barrett tells about a young brother and sister who had lost their parents. The older sister was taking care of her brother as he apparently was paralyzed on one side or possibly missing a limb.

How do they know? Barrett says sometimes it's a process of elimination in trying to figure these things out. When the brother's spirit answered through the dowsing rods, only one limb moved; the other stayed completely still. The group also relied on empathic team members and guests who reported feeling a heaviness on one side of their bodies, just like the young boy would have felt.

Unlike the other equipment, dowsing rods don't really measure anything but instead are communication devices relying on spiritual energy to make them move and provide answers. When the rods move to form a cross, the answer to the question is "yes." If they don't move or instead move apart, take it as a "no."

"The dowsing rods are only capable of answering questions that can be answered with a yes or no," she says. "So, we have to get very creative with our questions at times, but we have been able to get them to spell names and indicate dates."

Another important piece of equipment is an Electronic Voice Phenomena (EVP) designed to pick up voices and sounds that generally can't be heard by the human ear.

"Although there have been many investigations where we've heard audible answers to our questions," she says, "sometimes they pick up sounds we haven't heard."

Their EVP recordings taken in the basement also picked up a lot of voices as well as the sound of chains rattling.

Even in a place as crowded with visitors from the past as Bonaparte's Retreat, identifying who's who among the ghosts is actually pretty easy, says Barrett.

"Just ask them, they'll tell you," she says, noting that the investigators have various ways of finding out names.

"First, we ask them to tell us their names," she says. "We tell them to say it audibly and we have a little box that can record their voice. Many times, they do tell us their names. If we suspect a name, we will say it and may get a yes or no answer on the recorder, or an answer on the dowsing rods and/or flashing lights on an EMF meter. We like to get at least two techniques happening at the same time to validate the info. We have several intuitive [people] on the team who also come up with names and then [those] are validated after [the ghosts say] the name.

Well, it's not quite that easy. Ghost chats can be complicated and rather opaque. That's why, if all else fails, Paranormal 911 goes low-tech, relying on dowsing rods—yes, similar to the ones used to find water. They start off in a typical, easy, and conversational way by asking the spirit what their name is and trying to catch the response either by hearing the spoken words or catching the reply on one of their digital devices capable of picking up inaudible sounds. If that doesn't work, then the team pulls out the dowsing rods—no, not to hit the ghost out of exasperation—but to help them spell out the name. Investigators start letter by letter, making sure to record the responses as they go.

"I'll say, if your first name begins with the letter A, B, C, or D, please cross the rods. If they don't cross, I move on to the next set of letters. By the time you get the first three or four letters, you can usually figure out the name, then move on to the last name. Sometimes, if you have a client who recognizes the first name they'll already know the last name and so you can stop there.

"We'll ask what the year is currently for them—not us. We usually first ask if it's before 1900, then go from there. We narrow it down by decades, then by year in that decade. Then with their age, depending on the adult/child answer, we start by asking if they are above the age of twenty. If yes, then we ask if they're above the age of thirty, and so on. Also about who they are. Are you an adult? Are you a child? Male/female?"

Agreeing it's a time-consuming process, Barrett says it gets results.

That's a lot of dowsing rod activity and so Sean Barrett, Mary's husband, developed, through trial and error, what she describes as a complex—and proprietary—theory that ultimately is a much easier way than all those crossed dowsing rods to pinpoint the specific time frame when a spirit was alive. He's tested it numerous times to validate his findings by comparing them to the responses they've gotten using rods and recorders and also through their research, and the couple believes it's accurate.

The investigative team also saw orbs in the basement. These blobs, which are usually green when caught on camera, are rarely spiritual, says Barrett.

"The majority are dust particles, lint, moisture, insects, pollen, and other stuff that reflect light into the camera lens," she says.

So how do you tell it's a ghostly orb? According to Barrett, orbs that are spiritual in nature usually have a very direct path.

"We rarely declare an orb as proof of a spirit presence unless there is other evidence produced at the same time, such as a meter going off, temperature change, voice on the recorder and things like that," says Barrett, who likes to keep her investigations scientifically based.

Though Indiana had many residents who supported emancipation, the state and federal laws were such that these residents jeopardized their families, their lands, and even their freedom by helping escaping African Americans. But, despite that, a large number of slaves moved through the state in the years before and during the Civil War, and there were some three hundred sites in southeastern Indiana where people hid or helped runaway slaves.

Maps highlighting UGRR sites created by Perrin and Einhaus are available at the Ripley County Tourism Office in Versailles. We can't guarantee you'll come across a ghost, but it certainly helps to understand the milieu in which the UGRR flourished here.

Indiana was always a free state, but some were sympathetic to the Confederate cause and willing to help bounty hunters track down runaways. Towns with a large population of Quakers, known for their abolitionist beliefs, needed to be avoided. It was said in Ripley County, not far from Napoleon, that Cross Plains and Friendship, despite its name, were more likely to betray a slave in return for a bounty.

The old Union Flat Rock Baptist Church was organized in the home of Harvey Marshall with a covenant stating, "We cannot receive slaveholders into the church nor those who believe that slavery is right." Runaway slaves worshipped in both Marshall's house, now being restored by members of the Marshall family, and the 1859 church next door (now Union Church), both of which are part of the history of the UGRR.

There were also stops on scenic Otter Creek.

"They would ride the horses up and down the creek in water to be quiet," says Einhaus. "Not much has changed in

Historians have created five driving trails that follow the Underground Railroad routes. The Union Flat Rock Baptist Church, next to the home of Harvey Marshall, which is being restored by his family, was one UGRR stop. Photo courtesy of Kendal Miller.

that part of the county since back then. It pretty much is as it was."

Indeed, legend has it that in the quiet of a dark night, the sounds of horses neighing and the soft plod of their hooves in the waters of Otter Creek can still be heard.

Abolitionists Harmon Smith and Stephen Andrews are buried in the Otter Creek cemetery.

Historic Ripley County Courthouse Square in Versailles was the site of a major showdown in June 1844. Facing an angry crowd, attorney Stephen Harding stood on the courthouse steps and delivered an anti-slavery speech. Behind him the courthouse doors were barricaded, and the crowd, armed and violent, was surging toward him. Harding was saved by Jonathan Gordon, a fellow abolitionist, who broke into the courthouse and threw open the doors, urging people to let Harding speak. And so they did. Harding continued on with a speech still considered to be one of the most eloquent in the state's history.

What remains of a stretch of Old Michigan Road, once a major thoroughfare, just outside of Versailles, looks much as it did in the mid-1800s. To stand here is to see sights similar to those seen both by the slave catchers and their henchmen lying in wait and by African Americans making their way to freedom. Surely if you're quiet enough a ghost will come along soon.

TWO

Spirits of the Waters

THE RIVERS AND the Great Lakes were passages to freedom for runaway slaves. But islands also offered a place to secure Confederate soldiers, isolating them and cutting them off from chances to escape.

LAKE ERIE'S HAUNTED ISLAND

It isn't Union dead haunting the three-hundred-acre Johnson's Island isolated in the cold waters of Lake Erie, with Canada to the north and Ohio on its southern side. Said to be one of the most haunted Civil War cemeteries in the country, it was chosen as the site to build a prison for Confederate soldiers and received its first guests in 1862.

The island, located three miles out in Lake Erie north of Sandusky, while pretty and bucolic in the summer, was so frigidly cold in the winter that one Southern prisoner remarked, "It was just the place to convert visitors to the theological belief of the Norwegians that Hell has torments of cold instead of heat."

The sixteen-acre stockyard prison there was hastily constructed to hold one thousand, but as the war progressed, that number sometimes reached up to fifteen thousand. Like in most Civil War prisons, many died from the limited amount of food available, as well as from the intense winter cold, battle wounds, disease while having little access to medical care, and, occasionally, when prisoners disobeyed rules, bullets.

Escape was nearly impossible—rugged waters separated Johnson's Island from both Canada and Ohio, with the Union state also a hostile place where escapees could quickly be recaptured and sent back. One Christmas Eve a group of Confederates decided to escape by walking across the frozen waters. Whether they made it or not no one knows. Only twelve Confederate soldiers were known to have escaped and lived to tell about it—an amazingly small number.

To keep their spirits up, the captured soldiers often sang the tunes of the South, humming or whistling "Dixie." More than a century later, when Italian workers, many of whom couldn't even speak English, came to the island to mine the quarries, there were times when they'd all find themselves humming the same tune together, though many were from different countries and didn't even know the songs. What was that tune you were singing, the quarry superintendent demanded from them, obviously spooked by the song he'd heard. When the workers looked at him unknowingly, he told them it was "Dixie." Scared, many of the quarry workers boarded the first boat off the island, vowing never to come back. Years later, many recalled the strangeness of the haunted island and the way they had started humming a tune they didn't know.

Two hundred prisoners are buried in the Johnson's Island cemetery, but most likely there are other bodies here as well; the Italian workers discovered skeletons throughout the island.

None of the dead here seem to rest easily. Confederate soldiers walk among the tombstones and also in the nearby woods. Voices are heard even when no one is there. When it storms, the Confederates rise from their graves and, marching in step, head south. Ghostly battles take place, shots are fired, screams are heard, and the island is full of the sound of marching. A comradery of sorts occurs during Memorial Day celebrations, when the Civil War prisoners join the festivities, marching along with the living.

MACKINAC ISLAND
STRAITS OF MACKINAC

Talk about country club prisons. The privations of Johnson's Island were indeed harsh, but for the few Confederate sympathizers who found themselves on beautiful Mackinac Island, located where two Great Lakes, Michigan and Huron, converge, the only thing missing were tennis courts.

In a world where nothing seems to stay the same, Mackinac Island remains much as it was in 1897, when the island's leaders banned automobiles. For more than a century since, the sounds here have been the clip-clopping of horses' hooves on brick roads, the jingling of harnesses, and the forlorn horns of the ferries as they make their way from the mainland across the Straits of Mackinac.

An island of many ghosts, Mackinac was first a Native American trading and gathering place; its name translates to Big Turtle. From about 1680 until the 1800s, French fur traders settled here, working with Native Americans to supply the European and US demand for furs, including beaver pelts high in demand for such things as beaver top hats.

As a historic aside, in 1815 John Jacob Astor established the American Fur Company (AFC), located in the center of Market Street (the home is still there and is now part of the Mackinac State Historic Parks). The AFC housed the agent's home and clerks' quarters. The company warehouse was where

Fort Mackinac stands 150 feet above the Straits of Mackinac, providing protection from attacks as well as an advantageous lookout point to see approaching ships on the surrounding waters. Photo courtesy of Jane Simon Ammeson.

the furs were processed and trade goods were assembled. AFC also established a retail store around 1820 on the corner of Market and Fort Streets as an outlet where the company could sell surplus merchandise (just think—this might have been America's first outlet mall). It was a place for AFC employees, island residents, and soldiers from Fort Mackinac to do their shopping.

It was the British who built, in 1781, Fort Mackinac. Poised atop a 150-foot high limestone bluff, the fort's whitewashed ramparts offer panoramic views of the pretty island town and the harbor beyond.

The British and the Americans engaged in several bloody battles to capture and recapture the strategic island (its placement helped control access to Lake Michigan and swaths of the Northwest Territories). Now the fort is a tourist attraction where interpreters dressed in nineteenth-century garb fire cannons over the ramparts and shoot muskets on the green, and visitors can peer into the officers' quarters, barracks, and the bar and billiards room where the soldiers drank—a large bottle of Schlitz beer cost five cents back then. Lunch and dinner are served in the low-ceilinged Fort Mackinac Tea Room, which has its original wood planked floors, and the menu there reflects the foods eaten by the soldiers more than a century ago.

But by 1861, the fort was almost emptied, its value as an outpost no longer relevant. Until . . .

Fort Mackinac as a Civil War Prison
Mackinac State Historic Parks, September 3, 2012.

A year later, things began to change at the post. In early 1862, victorious Federal forces recaptured much of Tennessee from the Confederacy. Andrew Johnson (later Lincoln's Vice President, and ultimately the 17th President) was installed as the military governor of the state, a position he used to quickly arrest several prominent Confederate sympathizers. On Johnson's orders, Josephus (or Joseph) Conn Guild, George Washington Barrow, and William Giles Harding were placed under arrest and shipped north. Aware of Johnson's actions, Secretary of War Edwin Stanton made preparations to exile the three men to Fort Mackinac, where their influence and wealth could not help the Confederate cause.

Despite their status as prisoners, the three men apparently enjoyed a pleasantly boring summer on Mackinac. They were allowed to explore the island with a small guard detachment, and wrote of Mackinac's interesting geological formations and rich history. In their frequent letters home to Tennessee, Guild and Barrow both complimented Capt. Wormer for his kindness and dignity. Indeed, the prisoners received such liberal treatment that in early August, Col. William

Hoffman, the Commissary-General of Prisoners, reprimanded Wormer for failing to impose harsher restrictions upon the men.

As the summer drew to a close, the War Department reassessed the value of Fort Mackinac as a prison. Col. Hoffman recommended that the Stanton Guard be disbanded, as its men could be better used in the field. On September 10, the troops and prisoners departed Fort Mackinac, bound again for Detroit. The Stanton Guard formally mustered out and disbanded on September 25. Guild and Harding swore allegiance to the U.S. and were released on September 30, 1862, leaving only Barrow in custody. He was transferred to the more established military prison on Johnson's Island in Lake Erie, near Sandusky, Ohio. He remained in prison until March 1863 when he was released as part of a prisoner exchange.

http://www.mackinacparks.com/tag/civil-war

Long winters drove men to drink, which led to violent actions directed against themselves or others. Children and mothers died in childbirth, and many people died of disease and injury since medical care was practically nonexistent. As pretty as the island is today in the late spring to early fall, its winters would certainly take a toll in the times before furnaces and refrigeration. Even now, the winter population is only around five hundred. In the summer, there are more horses than that. So one would expect a multitude of spirits, a list that would include the pipers who play their mournful tunes from the fort's ramparts, French fur trappers still paddling their oversized canoes trapping beavers, the British and American dead who haunt the island and the fort, the young children in their Victorian-era clothing searching for their moms at some of the older hotels, brutally murdered Native Americans whose ghosts still hang out at the Stone Archway

A horse-driven lorry passes in front of what is now the Stuart House City Museum. The building was erected in 1817 for Robert Stuart, the resident agent for John Jacob Astor's American Fur Trading Post. Photo courtesy of Jane Simon Ammeson.

and the caves in the island's interior, sailors who didn't make it to shore alive, mothers still mourning their lost children, and turn-of-the-last-century guests who, foiled in love, decided to take too much laudanum.

Bullet wounds, scurvy, drownings—you name it, they died from it here. But the three Civil War prisoners fared well, even the one who ended up on Johnson's Island.

But ghosts of runaway slaves? How did that come to be?

Most likely because the Chicago-to-Mackinac-to-Duluth route was among the seven routes of the Underground Railroad in Michigan. This "railroad" passage follows the east coast of Lake Michigan up the western side of the state and crosses the Straits of Mackinac. The route then heads northwest toward Sault Ste. Marie, tracing the lower edge of

A cannon on the ramparts of Fort Mackinac overlooks the town and the harbor beyond. Photo courtesy of Jane Simon Ammeson.

Lake Superior toward Duluth. It's a long journey, the longest of any of the seven routes, which mostly lead to the cities of Detroit and Port Huron, then across Lake Huron into Canada. Or, if ghosts get to pick and choose where to be, why not this lovely island with its eighteenth-century downtown and magnificent grand hotel?

ALTON, ILLINOIS

Considered one of the most haunted towns in Illinois, Alton was a stop on the Underground Railroad for slaves traveling the Mississippi River, some of whom would settle in Illinois, a free state. Because it was just across the water from Missouri, where slavery was legal and the slave auctions held downriver in St. Louis, it was also where violence between pro- and antislavery forces was rife.

Elijah Parish Lovejoy Was Killed by a Pro-Slavery Mob

On November 7, 1837, Elijah Parish Lovejoy was killed by a pro-slavery mob while defending the site of his anti-slavery newspaper, *The Saint Louis Observer.* His death deeply affected many Northerners and greatly strengthened the abolitionist (antislavery) cause. Who was Lovejoy and why did his death cause such a strong reaction around the country?

Lovejoy, born in 1802, in Albion, Maine, sought his fortune in the Midwest after his college graduation. Over time, he became editor and part-owner of *The St. Louis Times.*

In 1832, caught up in the powerful religious revival movement sweeping the U.S., Lovejoy sold his business and went back East to study religion. There, a group of St. Louis businessmen recruited Lovejoy to return to St. Louis as editor of a new paper, *The Saint Louis Observer,* designed to promote religious and moral education. Supported by abolitionist friends such as Edward Beecher (the brother of Harriet Beecher Stowe, author of *Uncle Tom's Cabin*), he wrote anti-slavery editorials. Over time, Lovejoy's writing against slavery and in support of abolition became more strongly worded.

No sooner was the press off-loaded from the steamboat than a drunken mob formed and tried to set fire to the warehouse where it was stored. When Lovejoy ran out to push them away, someone shot him. Throughout the North and West, more people joined anti-slavery societies following Lovejoy's death. Officials in Illinois said almost nothing about the incident, with the exception of a young state representative named Abraham Lincoln, who spoke out against the crime.

> http://www.americaslibrary.gov/jb/reform
> /jb_reform_lovejoy_1.html

Abraham Lincoln visited Alton often, and here he and Stephen Douglas held one of their great debates. The home of

Senator Lyman Trumbull, author of the Thirteenth Amendment, which ended slavery in the United States, is a National Historic Landmark.

Trumbull is buried in the Alton City Cemetery. So is Lovejoy, who was murdered just steps away as he stood in front of the door of a mill, cradling a rifle to prevent his fourth printing press from being destroyed. He didn't save the press either—it was thrown into the Mississippi.

The cemetery also holds the bodies of Union soldiers who died during the Civil War.

At the top of a set of stone steps flanked by greenery and leading into the Alton Cemetery, a ninety-three-foot granite column topped with a winged statue of Victory honors Lovejoy's courage. His tomb, surrounded by a wrought iron fence, bears a Latin inscription reading "Here rests Lovejoy; Now spare this grave."

But Lovejoy may not be resting. His ghost is frequently seen around his gravesite, and, even on warm days, there are distinct cold spots. Also said to haunt in close proximity is the friendly spirit of nine-year-old Lucy Jane Haskell, the daughter of Dr. and Mrs. Haskell, one of the wealthiest families in Alton. Lucy Jane, who died of diphtheria in 1890, is reported to be a happy ghost who enjoys running and playing among the tombstones. Her sister, Florence, died four year later on October 1, 1894, just eight months after her birth. Florence for some reason seems content to stay in her grave; no hauntings by her have been reported. Another ghost haunting the cemetery is described as a lady in black who walks the hallway of the Grandview Public Mausoleum located inside the cemetery.

Not far away is the site of the state's first penitentiary, which opened in 1833. Used as a prisoner of war camp for captured Confederate soldiers, it was overcrowded and rampant with diseases.

Not a Country Club Prison

Mortality rate was above average for a Union prison. Hot, humid summers and cold Midwestern winters took a heavy toll on prisoners already weakened by poor nourishment and inadequate clothing. The prison was overcrowded much of the time and sanitary facilities were inadequate. Pneumonia and dysentery were common killers but contagious diseases such as smallpox and rubella were the most feared. When smallpox infection became alarmingly high in the winter of 1862 and spring of 1863, a quarantine hospital was located on an island across the Mississippi River from the prison.

Up to 300 prisoners and soldiers died and were buried on the island in the river, now under water. A cemetery in North Alton that belonged to the State of Illinois was used for most of the dead. A monument there lists 1,534 names of Confederate soldiers that are known to have died.

http://www.altonweb.com/history/civilwar/confed/

After the prison was closed, its stones were used in the construction of other buildings throughout the city, most likely spreading more ghostly visitations.

With the dead from both sides of the Civil War—Confederate and Union—Reverend Lovejoy, the lady dressed in black, and little Lucy, there's a long list of ghosts who spend their time at the cemetery.

But Alton has even more hauntings, many dating back to its days as a stop on the Underground Railroad.

"This town is interesting because it's so historic," says Becky Nelson of the Alton Visitor's Center. "And there are a lot of people who live here and who come from all over the country who believe in the hauntings. The largest national gathering of a paranormal society meets here. We have lots and lots of ghost tours."

Nelson says she took one of the Underground Railroad tours.

Also, when she was growing up she had one friend who lived in one of the large mansions near the river where there were tunnels in the basement, most likely used as a place for slaves to hide during the Underground Railroad days.

THE ENOS SANITARIUM

SANITARIUM for the TREATMENT OF ALL CURABLE DISEASES.
Alton Telegraph, Thursday, May 22, 1890

"It was a mansion at one time that was turned into apartments; my sister lived there and she took me down to the laundry area," says Nelson. "The tunnels were right there and they go all the way down to the river and to the boats. Looking at them, I kept thinking about those poor people trying to escape."

Built in 1857 by Nathaniel Hanson, the mansion was designed, just like the Levi Coffin home in Fountain City, as a station on the UGRR. It's located on a bluff overlooking the Mississippi River, and Hanson was said to have workers construct tunnels leading from the basement and under Third Street. Similar to the Slippery Noodle Inn in Indiana, which was also constructed to accommodate slaves, the basement was extra deep and had many small rooms and narrow hallways carved out of the limestone it's built upon. Supposedly, the cupola on top of the Hanson Mansion could be used to signal runaways arriving on the Mississippi. One light meant all clear and two meant danger. High enough, the signals could be seen from the Missouri side of the Mississippi as well.

The hauntings connected to the UGRR take place in the basement, where the tunnels are located. But like in many old places with lots of history, there are other spirits here as well. Upstairs the ghosts most likely belonged to its residents, first family members and then, in 1911 and beyond, others who came here to get well after Dr. W. H. Enos purchased the mansion, added a fourth floor and a side structure, and opened the Enos Sanitarium, which catered to people with tuberculosis.

Many of those traveling along the UGRR were sick, hungry, cold, and ill, and often perished on the way. Also, tuberculosis was incurable before the invention of penicillin, and by the time someone was ill enough to need the treatments of a sanitarium (lots of fresh air and rest being the most that could be offered), their chance of survival was very poor. At the beginning of the nineteenth century, tuberculosis had killed one in seven of all people who had ever lived. One hundred years later it was still a deadly disease with an estimated 110,000 Americans dying each year from tuberculosis.

With so many fatalities in the area, there's bound to be a lot of ghostly activity in Alton, and so there is. Objects fly through the air, there are the sounds of something crashing, footsteps can be heard when no one is there, doors open and close on their own, and lights flicker on and off. Mysterious shadows, things disappearing only to reappear later in different places, areas of unexpected cold, and the appearance of a ghostly young boy are also common occurrences.

In his book *Alton Hauntings*, author Troy Taylor, who also runs the Alton Haunting Ghost Tours, recounts what happened to a couple he had interviewed who had lived there. Hearing knocking on the basement door, they'd open it to find no one there. Late at night the two would awake to footsteps outside of their bedroom in the hallway, but— you guessed it—there was no one there. Sometimes a pungent odor like a dead animal would float through the air.

These hauntings escalated until the couple would hear a choking cry coming from all directions, including from under their bed.

GHOSTS IN THE CITY
DOWNTOWN CLEVELAND, OHIO

Narrow stairs lead down to the brick-lined tunnels beneath the Cuyahoga County Soldiers and Sailors Monument at Public Square in downtown Cleveland. Dark and damp, the serpentine underground passageways are a stark contrast to the ornate ground-level monument, all gilt and marble, and the 125-foot polished black Quincy-granite shaft topped by a bronze statue of the Goddess of Freedom defended by the Shield of Liberty. More bronze statues grouped around the base portray the four branches of the Union Army—the navy, cavalry, infantry, and artillery. The monument acknowledges the dedication of the 325,000 Ohio soldiers who fought in the war—the third-largest contingent behind New York and Pennsylvania among the Union states.

Said to be haunted by Civil War soldiers, the tunnels seem like they might have been made just for ghosts, but the real reason for their existence is more prosaic. The circular system supports all the weight of the monument above. Paranormal societies who've investigated down there have observed a myriad of ghostly manifestations—orbs, voices, and overall feelings of unearthly presences.

LEGENDS OF THE DUNES

Today hikers can take the relatively easy 2.1-mile Chellberg Farm and Bailly Homestead Trail loop at the Indiana Dunes National Lakeshore and visit (when it's open for tours) the homestead of Joseph Bailly, a French Canadian fur trader

Ghosts of Civil War soldiers haunt the dark and dank tunnels beneath the Cuyahoga County Soldiers and Sailors Monument in downtown Cleveland. Photo courtesy of Detroit Publishing and the Library of Congress.

Alton's riverfront location along the Mississippi River made it a crucial stop for slaves seeking to make connections to freedom in the northern United States and Canada. Alton, considered one of the most haunted cities in Illinois and the surrounding areas, had many safe houses. Tunnels under the Enos Apartments are haunted still by the ghosts of runaway slaves. Photo courtesy of Alton Regional Convention and Visitors Bureau.

who came to northwest Indiana in 1822 when it was still an almost impenetrable wilderness. Bailly built a trading post on the Little Calumet River where the Pottawatomi and Sauk India trails converged. Later it would also become a stagecoach stop. At its earliest, it was one of only two posts between Fort Dearborn, which later became Chicago, and Detroit. The homestead's isolated setting made it good hiding place for slaves and their ghosts, which are still said to haunt the marshes, woods, and towering sand dunes.

Though she has no connection to runaway slaves, the Civil War, or the Underground Railroad, the most well-known ghost of the southern Lake Michigan shoreline is Diana of the Dunes, a free spirit even in life.

Alton's Union Baptist Church, one of the oldest black churches in Illinois, was founded by free Blacks around the 1820s. John Livingstone, Union Baptist's founding pastor, was the pressman for abolitionist newspaper editor Elijah P. Lovejoy, who was murdered in 1837 by an anti-abolitionist mob. Lovejoy, who still wanders the areas by his tombstone and a monument in his honor at the Alton City Cemetery, was lauded by then state senator Abraham Lincoln. Photo courtesy of Alton Regional Convention and Visitors Bureau.

Diana of the Dunes Fled from World of Men: Discloses Mysteries of Weird Life to Woman Writer.

Garbed in Sailcloth, Disillusioned Graduate of Chicago University is Finding "Peace That the City Cannot Give" in Indiana Wilderness.

Here on the shore of Lake Michigan, in the foothills of high sand dunes, in a wilderness of pine trees and a jungle of marshes, miles beyond the echo of human voice, I found "Diana of the Dunes," Alice Gray, University of Chicago graduate who, since last October has spoken less than a dozen times to human creatures!

Diana of mythology was known to the Romans as the chaste goddess—Diana the huntress. She hated men and went into the wilderness to live in Virgin purity.

Joseph Bailly, a French Canadian fur trader, built a trading post in what is now the Indiana Dunes National Lakeshore. Later it was also a stagecoach stop and a station on the Underground Railroad. Ghosts of Native Americans, early settlers, runaway slaves, and a free spirit called Diana of the Dunes are all said to haunt the lakeshore. Interestingly, in the early 1900s, the dunes were also used in silent movies as a stand-in for the deserts of Sudan. Photo courtesy of Westchester Township Historical Society.

This Diana in the flesh, I found hedged from the world by two miles of last impenetrable sand drifts and boggy marshes. And it was through these drifts and marshes that I traveled— the first woman to penetrate the sanctuary of this modern-world Diana who has just been discovered by fishermen in solitude as deep as the solitude of Alexander Selkirk on his desert isle.

It was dawn when I came upon her retreat in the dunes. The hut was empty but a bed of green boughs and two sinister revolvers on the floor of the bed was assurance I had found the hermit's hiding place. When a strong, lithe, clear-eyed smiling young woman, bare legged as a nymph, hair cut boy fashion, face sun kissed to a deep brown, spring through pine scrub, I knew I had found "Diana."

... "I was working in Chicago, making little in the way of money, doing little in the importance in the world, it seemed. I had measured myself with the world—the results were not encouraging. I came here to measure myself with nature.

"I found a cave here in the hills, spread my blanket, slept under the stars and communed with myself. I began to live . . . ."

Her name is Alice Gray. She graduated from the University of Chicago in 1903; held a secretaryship in a large publishing house and it was predicted she would follow a literary career . . .

She has heard of the Sahara-like sand dunes that drift along the lake shore. To the dunes she came. There was no human habitation in sight. In a dugout she spread her blanket.

"The dug out was too cold," she says, "and I found this hut.

"Everything I have here, this chair, the cap I wear . . . are drift wool, drifted in from the lake—I too am driftwood.

"I got the sail's cloth from a fisherman and made this thing I wear. I got rid of everything that looked like the city.

"The fisherman who live way up the beach sometime bring some extra too . . . boys sell me eggs. I have reduced the cost of living to almost nothing—10 cents a day at most.

"Someday I suppose I'll want to go back. But the city can never give me what the wilderness has given me—peace of mind and the strength of mind to live alone."

Fort Wayne Weekly Sentinel (Fort Wayne, Indiana),
Tuesday, August 1, 1916
By Honor Fanning

Alice Gray never did return to the city but unfortunately she didn't stay away from the world of men, bad men, that is.

Find Man Dead in Sand Dunes of Indiana: Police Hunt "Diana of the Dunes" as Clue to Death of Unidentified Man.

The finding of the body of an unidentified man, charred beyond recognition in the sand dunes eight miles east of Chesterton, Indiana, today has provided the authorities of Porter County, Indiana, with a grim mystery from which sensational disclosures are expected.

"Diana of the Dunes," a woman who has lived in half barbaric style on the dunes for the past eight years and a man known as "Wilson," who is said to have posed as the husband of Diana, were linked with the mystery when the police started in search of them. Neither has been seen for several days.

Logansport Pharos-Tribune (Logansport, Indiana),
Friday, June 9, 1922

Well-to-Do Camper

The body of the man, a rifle clutched in his hand, was found late yesterday. From all appearances the man was a well-to-do camper. In a satchel near the body was a complete radio set and an expensive camping outfit . . . From the date of the purchase tickets and a copy of a newspaper found beneath the body, the man is believed to have left Chicago May 29. The condition of the body indicates he has been dead nearly that long.

Logansport Pharos-Tribune, June 9, 1922

May Be Ex-Convict

The man known as "Wilson" whom the authorities are seeking, is said to have come to the dunes comparatively recently and to have taken up his habitation in the hut occupied by

"Diana." He and "Diana" became familiar characters about the dunes and the beach that skirts them. Authorities say their records indicate that Wilson is an ex-convict.

"Diana of the Dunes" and "Husband" Hurt in a Fight

Her skull fractured by a blow from the butt of a revolver, Mrs. Alice Gray Wilson, known as "Diana of the Dunes," is in a hospital at Gary, Indiana, today. Physicians regard her injury as serious.

Frank Wilson, her husband, is suffering from a bullet wound in his foot and Eugene Frank, a boatman, is under arrest charged with inflicting the wounds upon "Diana" and her husband.

Frank claims that Wilson's jealousy over "Diana" caused an attack on him by Wilson and that "Diana" joined in the assault. He struck with the gun and fired at Wilson, Frank claims, in self-defense.

Other residents of the sand dunes declared that the trouble was engendered by resentment felt by Wilson and his wife over stories circulated that they were connected with the death of the unknown camper, the finding of whose body has furnished the dunes with an absorbing mystery.

Huntington Herald (Huntington, Indiana), Wednesday,
June 14, 1922
By International News Service

In 1925, Gray was dead from uremic poisoning.

The *Chesterton Tribune* reported in its February 19, 1925, issue that Wilson drew a pistol in the midst of the funeral services and threatened to kill two men, one of whom was a newspaperman. He was taken to the police station and couldn't attend the rest of the service. By the next year, he reportedly was married to another woman and was arrested during a hold-up on U.S. 6 before being shot dead during another burglary.

Diana continues to haunt the dunes and is often seen at night, skinny-dipping as she did when she was alive. Whether she's ever joined by the ghosts of runaway slaves, we don't know. But it's nice to imagine a gathering of spirits enjoying the beauty of a silvery moon reflected on the waters of Lake Michigan.

THREE

Sold down the River

The Reverse Underground Railroad

SLAVERY'S ATTIC: DOES HISTORIC MANSION HOLD A DARK PAST OR A FAMILY'S RICH HERITAGE?
Chicago Tribune, July 08, 1991

John Crenshaw drew most of his wealth and influence from his government contracts to produce salt from the Gallatin Salines, natural salt springs and brine deposit licks that were a leading source of salt for Illinois and the nation in the early 1800s. The industry profited white men like Crenshaw, but it was powered mostly by slave labor.

Salt-making operations required more manpower than was otherwise available, so black slaves from Kentucky and Tennessee, as well as indentured servants and freedmen, were rented from their owners or hired by Crenshaw and others who held the (salt) leases.

At peak production, Crenshaw's salt works near Lower Lick Spring and Half Moon Lick employed nearly 1,000. The use of slave labor was so important to the lucrative salt-works, which at one point paid one-seventh of all state taxes, that the first Illinois Constitution of 1818 prohibited slave labor everywhere in the state except at the Gallatin Salines.

Most local historians and Crenshaw's descendants, including members of the prominent Lanphier family in Springfield, do not dispute that the original owner of the Hickory Hill mansion used slave labor legally in his business.

But they have been outraged by (then owner) Sisk's claim that he kidnapped, tortured and bred them, even though there is some historical data to support Sisk's claims.

There is no mumbo jumbo in court records showing that in 1842, Crenshaw was indicted along with the notorious "Negro-napper" Hardin Kuykendall for illegal slave trading in Gallatin County, where southern slaves seeking freedom often crossed the Ohio River into Illinois at Old Shawneetown.

Crenshaw was acquitted, however, because of insufficient evidence.

His descendants said that he was framed by his enemies. Sisk said Crenshaw was acquitted because witnesses were afraid to testify against him.

Evidence Bolsters Case for Old Slave House

The three researchers, Ron Nelson, Jon Musgrave and Gary DeNeal, say the discoveries made just last week clinches their previous findings that John Hart Crenshaw, builder of the Old Slave House, profited not only from his salt works, but his major illegal operations involving the kidnapping of free blacks, indentured servants and improperly held slaves, in order to sell them back into slavery.

"The findings occurred almost by accident," said Nelson, a long-time historian of southeastern Illinois. "I was in the Illinois State Historical Library wanting copies of some letters we already had transcripts of, when I came across a second letter in the Frank Granger case that nearly blew me away."

Crenshaw's kidnapping of Frank Granger, a black man illegally held as a slave in Illinois, took place in about 1827 and represents the earliest identifiable victim the researchers have found. The new letter found a week ago Monday, followed up on the first letter and listed another 15 victims in the same situation as Frank.

"That's important because it more than doubles the number of victims we have who are identified by contemporary documents. These aren't statistics, but real people whose plight is being described in letters written on their behalf," explained Jon Musgrave, owner of IllinoisHistory.com.

"We have about 30 victims identified by names in these early letters. In addition, there are another four who were identified more than a century later as Crenshaw's kidnapped victims. In one letter we even discovered that Crenshaw tried to help a group of slave traders with a lawsuit trying to lay claim to more than 22 freed slaves plus their descendants," Musgrave added.

Besides just adding to the quantity of Crenshaw's crimes, the researchers said the newly discovered letter as well documents found last Tuesday and Wednesday in Tennessee, shift the focus to Crenshaw's early involvement in the kidnapping trade.

"These two letters date back to the year Crenshaw and his brother bought Hickory Hill, the site of the Old Slave House. We have long said it appeared that Crenshaw purchased the land from his kidnapping operations. The sale of Frank Granger and the others would have likely netted Crenshaw around $5,200, if not more, based on a price of $400 per adult and $200 per child," said Musgrave.

"To put this in perspective, the state sold land back then for 50 cents to $2 an acre. A 10-year-old kid was worth $200, which could have been used to buy 400 acres of land," Musgrave added.

IllinoisHistory.com, September 28, 1999

Crenshaw wasn't the only operator on the Reverse Underground Railroad in both Indiana and Illinois.

Another mansion south of Shawneetown also was a station on the reverse UGRR. Here victims were imprisoned in cells in the basement, most likely shackled to the large iron rings set into the walls of each cell. Slaves were also said to be kept by one of Shawneetown's prominent residents, a man identified as "Mr. John C," in a cave near his home.

Black Kidnappings in the Wabash and Ohio Valleys of Illinois

The kidnapping of free blacks had long been a problem in Illinois. The Black Code of 1819 allowed a fine of $1000 to be levied on behalf of the victim but did not provide for any criminal convictions. Coupled with the fact that blacks could not testify in court against a white man, the two made any legal remedy almost useless. Only in a few counties where the pro-slaver sentiment wasn't so strong did free blacks win cases against white kidnappers. Usually it was for the crime of trespass and only with the help of friendly whites did they convince juries.

By Jon Musgrave. Oak Hill Plantation
Preservation Project, April–May 1997

Crenshaw, who lived near the town of Equality in Gallatin County, Illinois, and his conspirators were selling free blacks "down the river" by forging papers identifying them as slaves and taking them deep into the south where they were beyond help.

Indeed, the term "sold down the river" originated during the time when slavery was legal, though it also referred to difficult slaves, such as those who tried to escape or made demands, who were sold to owners further south or downriver, where it was much more difficult to escape to a northern free state.

Crenshaw also supposedly kept African Americans enslaved at his Hickory Hill mansion in Southern Illinois just across the river from Kentucky, at first exploiting a law that let slaves be used to work in the labor-intensive salt mines and, when the law expired, not letting them leave. Rumors were rife about the horrors of Hickory Hill—or the Old Slave House, as it was nicknamed—and include stories about imprisonment on the third floor of the house, forced pregnancies to increase the "stock" of slaves to be sold, and violence to keep them in line.

Though the first two floors, each with six rooms, of the Greek Revival–style mansion were opulently and expensively furnished during the time that Crenshaw (who also went by the name of Granger), his wife, and their children lived there, the third floor with its thick walls and small windows had a different type of decor—whipping posts, cells about the size of horse stalls, metal rings, chains, and barred doors. Entrance was via a passage in the back of the house large enough for a wagon transporting kidnapped freed blacks and indentured whites to enter. Taken to the third floor, they were said to be raped, tortured, beaten, and, at times, though it must have cut into profits, even murdered. A tunnel connected the home to the river where prisoners either arrived or were shipped to southern slave states.

It's no wonder Hickory Hill is said to be haunted.

Operators of the reverse UGRR were a rough, heartless group of men. Jon Musgrave, who has studied the subject extensively, tells of a James Lynch, who in late 1835 or early 1836 was on his way from Shawneetown to Equality to file emancipation papers for a family slave when he disappeared.

In Pope County, known kidnapper Caleb Slankard operated a gang that abducted blacks. His boss, or partner, at one time was William H. Vaughn, a Bay City storekeeper. Vaughn was believed to have been a pirate on the Gulf Coast before moving to his storeboat in the Ohio River. He was tied to at least two kidnappings involving a total of several children. After he testified as a grand jury that Slankard and others had actually done the abduction, he died from an unexpected seizure. It was believed someone poisoned his whiskey.

As an aside—isn't Slankard the perfect name for a man engaged in such hideous practices?

Slankard, who had been a river pirate before turning to the lucrative business of kidnapping free blacks was married to the daughter of Samuel Hazel. Overall, one might assume from the following newspaper article, dated Wednesday, July 22, 1874, that they weren't the kindest-hearted group of people.

A Pope County Mystery

Samuel Hazel of Pope County, who was insane for a number of years, came to his death in a mysterious and horrible manner. He had been an inmate of the insane asylum at Anna for some months past. A few weeks ago, his brother, also living in Pope County, was notified that his removal from the asylum had become necessary and accordingly went after him.

When within a few miles of their home in Pope County, the two stopped at a farm house to stay overnight. Before morning the unfortunate escaped the vigilant eye of his brother, and no trace of him could be found until last week when his body was found in the bushes near the Johnson County line. His death was evidently the result of foul work.

His body, which had been partly devoured by swine, was minus the head and right arm. The head was found about fifteen feet from the body and from its appearance must have been cut off with some instrument. The arm could not be found.

The inducement for the vile deed is supposed to have been money, as the murdered man is said to have had some about his person, and report points to a relative as the perpetrator; but this is probably more conjecture. The affair is sufficiently horrible whoever may have committed the deed or whatever may have been the motive.

Cairo Daily Bulletin (Cairo, Illinois), Wednesday July 22, 1874

But then, what else would you expect from people involved in a big business whose success resulted in the misery, imprisonment, and even death of men, women, and children?

Researchers like Musgrave say that many records have disappeared over the years, destroyed by fires and floods or just missing. Fortunately, newspaper archives and surviving court documents tell the horrific stories of the kidnapping of free blacks, including little children who were then taken across the Ohio and Mississippi rivers and sold as slaves.

WAS KIDNAPPED, in the neighborhood of the Saline, a NEGRO GIRL, named Maria, about eight years of age, dark complexion, nearly black, well grown of her age, has a dent or small hole in her face just below the cheek bone; she had strings in her ears, though the Thieves may use the precaution to take them out, her ears however have been pierced, and they cannot destroy that mark. The clothes she had on when taken off were very ragged, and it is presumed will soon be changed. She was taken from the spring on Saturday evening the 25th inst. by two ruffians who are unknown. This girl is one of the negroes emancipated by the last will and testament of John McAllister, of Montgomery County, Tennessee and moved here about a year ago, and sometime last spring some scoundrel— probably one of these—stole two horse creatures from them, and thereby prevented them from making a crop, and now returned to steal the children. The uncle of the girl, a black man of the name of DRYAS, offers a reward of FIFTY DOLLARS for the girl, and a Subscription is now making up for the Girl and Thief or Thieves, and I am of opinion that TWO HUNDRED DOLLARS will be raised.

LEO D. WHITE, 27th July 1829

A Handsome Reward: Ran away or was kidnapped off the plantation of the subscriber, on Monday, the 4th inst. a bright Mulatto Boy, named, Madison George; about 11 years of age, small of his age; his face somewhat marked from a burn; and sore eyes. Had on when he disappeared a muslin shirt, and tow linen pantaloons. When spoken to, is apt to smile.

I will give the Eighty acres of Land that I now reside on, which is my all, and is clear of all encumbrance, for the recovery of the Boy, and conviction of the Thief—or $10 for the Boy alone.

JOHN LOCKHART
Gallatin County, Ill. Sept. 8, 1826

Hickory Hills, situated on the Saline River, was bought by the Sisk family in 1906, and in 1930 they started marketing it with an emphasis on the home's gruesome history and hauntings. And indeed there are many. Visitors report the sounds of rattling chains, moans and wailing, the unwelcome touch of unseen entities, and cold spots. Over time, the upkeep on the house, listed on the National Register of Historic Places, became too expensive, and it fell into disrepair. Now it's the property of the Illinois Historic Preservation Agency, and funds are being sought to restore it.

It's interesting to note, when reading the history of Hickory Hill, that though Illinois was a free state, because it was hard to find free laborers (most likely because employers weren't willing to pay enough) to work in the salt mines, the state had a special exemption, and Crenshaw was allowed to lease slaves from other states, such as Kentucky. At one time he had almost eight hundred slaves working for him in the mines.

In a macabre aside, Crenshaw's great-great-grandson was Joe Ball, a Texas bootlegger said to have murdered at least two women, including a girlfriend and his wife, and possibly up to twenty more. Ball owned a bar called the Sociable Inn, which sounds anything but. Part of the inn's decor were six alligators swimming in a large pool. In 1938, when authorities tried to interview him about the missing women, Ball, who served in World War I, pulled a revolver from the cash register and shot himself in the head. His handyman and accessory to the crimes led authorities to the bodies of two women, telling the police that Joe had killed a total of twenty or so but that the alligators had eaten the evidence. If true, apparently some apples really don't fall far from the tree.

Another anecdote tells how Crenshaw's brutal beating of several female slaves so enraged several male slaves held nearby that they were able to break their restraints and, rushing him, cut off one of his legs. A photo taken of Crenshaw and his wife at a later date shows him holding a crutch on his lap.

Just desserts if it's true.

FOUR

Lincoln Walks at Midnight

IN 1865, WHEN mourners watched as the last railroad car, the one carrying the bodies of Abraham Lincoln and his young son, disappeared from view, most thought it was a sight never to be seen again.

A logical premise, but one that was wrong.

More than a million people turned out to watch the Lincoln Express make that final journey from Washington D.C. to Springfield, where Lincoln was laid to rest.

Those numbers keep rising through the decades, as the wheels of the funeral train keep rolling, following its original schedule, and mourners can still see the locomotive emerge from a dark fog that falls upon the scene. As it pulls into view, with the sounds of mournful music wafting through the air, mourners see a true skeleton crew driving and ghostly Union soldiers standing guard around the coffin of their fallen commander in chief.

The train pulled into Cleveland on April 28 at 6:50 a.m. at Monument Square and stayed until the next evening when it left for Columbus, Ohio, at midnight. There the coffin was carried to the state house, while more than fifty thousand mourners waited for the chance to pay their respects. From

Columbus, the train passed through Saint Paris, Piqua, and Urbana as it headed toward Indiana. After a stopover in Indianapolis, the train continued north, traveling through Whitestown, Lebanon, Francesville, Medaryville, San Pierre, Wanatah, and Westville. In Michigan City, as the train pulled into the station at 8 a.m. on May 1, residents proudly showed off their memorial to the president—a thirty-feet-high, twenty-feet-wide evergreen archway dotted with roses and mourning banners expressing such heartfelt sentiments as "With tears we resign thee to God and history" and "Abraham Lincoln, noblest martyr to freedom."

From Chicago, the train turned south on May 2 at 9:30 p.m. and reached Springfield, Illinois, its final destination, at 9 a.m. the next morning.

Want to pay your respects? Choose the time and place where the train passed more than a century-and-half ago and wait. As it arrives, clocks and watches stop and later, when it's gone they restart and it's as though time has never passed.

The ghost portrait of Abraham Lincoln can be seen at the Lincoln Financial Foundation Collection at the Allen County Public Library in Fort Wayne, Indiana. Taken in 1872 by William Mumier, a spirit photographer, it shows Mary Todd Lincoln dressed in her widow's garb with the ghostly outline of her husband standing behind her, his hands protectively resting on her shoulders. What adds to its authenticity, or so the story goes, is that Mumier supposedly didn't know who the woman sitting for the photograph was until right before the picture was taken. Mumier, later prosecuted for fraud, was acquitted but his career was pretty much destroyed. Poor Mary didn't fare much better. Life had worn her down—two sons lost and a husband brutally murdered. She relied on spiritualism and loved the portrait, which indicated to her that reunification with her lost loved ones waited

Abraham Lincoln at his home in Springfield, Illinois, with a large crowd of people gathered outside after a Republican rally, August 8, 1860. The spirits of both Lincoln and his wife, Mary, are said to haunt the house. Photo courtesy of the Library of Congress.

ahead at some future time. She was tried for insanity but won her case. But still . . . how much can a woman bear?

HAUNTINGS IN SPRINGFIELD

"Actual ghost stories are subjective, and have no doubt been exaggerated over the years," says Garret Moffett, owner of Springfield Walks & Tour Guide Services, who conducts a twelve-block Lincoln's Ghost Walk encompassing many of the places Lincoln frequented while living there, such as the Lincoln-Herndon law office at the corner of Sixth and Adams Streets, the home where the Lincolns lived, and, of course, his tomb.

"My stories are researched to be the most accurate and tend to come from people that knew Lincoln personally rather than from someone who never met the man," continues

Moffett. "The funeral train stories are the perfect example. I have no doubt that in 1865 people might have encountered a ghostly train or at least the sounds of a ghostly train and maybe even continues today, and I can relate and use those stories. But the stories now involve a vivid sighting of the train as it silently thunders past, and people claim seeing a skeleton honor guard surrounding Lincoln's coffin. To me that part is unbelievable so I don't use that in my stories."

Moffett instead focuses on Lincoln's involvement in spiritualism.

"The ghost stories of Lincoln have more to do with the Lincolns' involvement with the Spiritualist movement of the day and the tragedies that surrounded the Lincolns," continues Moffett, who has always had an avid interest in Lincoln and began intensively studying his life about fifteen years ago. "But there are stories of Lincoln haunting the White House, the tomb site, and the streets of Springfield. There are stories about Mary in the house as well."

It was just after my election in 1860—I was well tired out, and went home to rest, throwing myself down on a lounge in my chamber. Opposite where I lay was a bureau, with a swinging-glass upon it and, looking in that glass, I saw myself reflected, nearly at full length; but my face, I noticed, had two separate and distinct images, the tip of the nose of one being about three inches from the tip of the other. I was a little bothered, perhaps startled, and got up and looked in the glass, but the illusion vanished. On lying down again I saw it a second time—plainer, if possible, than before; and then I noticed that one of the faces was a little paler, say five shades, than the other. I got up and the thing melted away, and I went off and, in the excitement of the hour, forgot all about it—nearly, but not quite, for the thing would once in a while come up, and give me a little pang, as though something uncomfortable had happened. When I went home I told my wife about it, and a few days after I tried the experiment again, when, sure enough, the thing came again; but I never succeeded in bringing the ghost back after that, though I once tried very industriously to show it to my wife, who was worried about it somewhat. She thought it was a sign that I was to be elected to a second term of office, and that the paleness of one of the faces was an omen that I should not see life through the last term.

Mary, who often held séances, had even more of a spiritualist world view, but the dreams foretelling Lincoln's death were disturbing to the president. Several weeks before John Wilkes Booth fired that fatal shot, Lincoln had another disturbing dream, which his former law partner, Ward Hill Lamon, transcribed in his book, *Recollections of Abraham Lincoln.*

About ten days ago, I retired very late. I had been up waiting for important dispatches from the front. I could not have been long in bed when I fell into a slumber, for I was weary. I soon began to dream. There seemed to be a deathlike stillness about me.

Then I heard subdued sobs, as if a number of people were weeping. I thought I left my bed and wandered downstairs. There the silence was broken by the same pitiful sobbing, but the mourners were invisible. I went from room to room; no living person was in sight, but the same mournful sounds of distress met me as I passed along. I saw light in all the rooms; every object was familiar to me; but where were all the people who were grieving as if their hearts would break?

I was puzzled and alarmed. What could be the meaning of all this? Determined to find the cause of a state of things so mysterious and so shocking, I kept on until I arrived at the East Room, which I entered. There I met with a sickening surprise.

Before me was a catafalque, on which rested a corpse wrapped in funeral vestments. Around it were stationed soldiers who were acting as guards. There was a throng of people, gazing mournfully upon the corpse, whose face was covered, others weeping pitifully.

"Who is dead in the White House?" I demanded of one of the soldiers. "The President," was his answer. "He was killed by an assassin." Then came a loud burst of grief from the crowd, which woke me from my dream. I slept no more that night; and although it was only a dream, I have been strangely annoyed by it ever since.

On the day he was assassinated, Lincoln asked his bodyguard, William H. Crook:

"Crook, do you know I believe there are men who want to take my life? And I have no doubt they will do it . . . I know no one could do it and escape alive. But if it is to be done, it is impossible to prevent it."

Not surprisingly, paranormal activity is ever present at Lincoln's tomb. Besides hauntings by the president's ghost, real macabre events such as several attempts by grave robbers to steal his body have occurred, including one shortly after he was interred.

Conspiracy to Steal Lincoln's Body

Santa Fe, N.M.—Terrence Mullen died suddenly while at work in a mine of the southern part of Santa Fe County a few days ago. He was a former citizen of Illinois and in 1865 formed a conspiracy to steal Abraham Lincoln's body from the grave and hold it for a ransom. For this he served a term in the Illinois State Prison. In 1888 he became involved in land frauds at San Marcial and went to the territorial penitentiary for two years.

Decatur Weekly Republican (Decatur, Illinois),
Thursday, March 18, 1897

People gathered around the crate containing the coffin of President Abraham Lincoln, April 30, 1901. In the background is his empty grave. There were many rumors and reports that Lincoln actually wasn't buried in his grave, which may be another reason why his spirit is said to haunt his tomb—he just doesn't know where to go. Photo courtesy of the Library of Congress.

Lincoln's Body

A Sensational Story That It Has Been Removed from the Sarcophagus for Safety.

An Official Denial and Statement of Facts.

A correspondent has made a discovery which will interest men and women where the name of Abraham Lincoln is spoken or his memory revered. The sarcophagus in which the remains of the martyr president were placed is empty. After satisfying himself of the truth of the statement, the reporter approached a gentleman who is perfectly cognizant of the action taken by the local monument committee and made known his discovery. The gentleman expressed no surprise as he remarked:

"Yes, Lincoln's body has been removed from the sarcophagus."

"Where is the body now?"

"I cannot tell."

"Do you know?"

"I can say that the body is safe."

"When did the removal take place?"

"That does not matter. It only concerns the public of this country to know that the body of Abraham Lincoln has been deposited where no ghoulish hands can ever desecrate it."

"What prompted the removal?"

"After attempts to steal the body had been made by grave robbers a few years ago, the parties who are responsible for the safe keeping of Mr. Lincoln's remains held a consultation and the proposition to remove the body from the sarcophagus was unanimously concurred in. It was the desire of those citizens and officials who assumed responsibility for the removal that the fact not be made public."

Pantagraph (Bloomington, Illinois), Friday, November 16, 1883

According to the article, Lincoln's body remained in the monument but in a place "where it will never be molested by grave robbers."

Right below this article was a letter from J. C. Power, custodian of the monument.

The Story Denied—An Official Statement

The remains have never been removed from the monument.

But Power wasn't telling the truth, at least according to legend. Lincoln's body had been moved to a tunnel connecting Memorial Hall and an underground labyrinth beneath the cemetery. Because of water seepage and the difficulty of digging a new grave undetected, Power and several other men simply covered his coffin with boards, leaving it there for several years.

When Mary Lincoln died, her coffin was placed next to Lincoln's, and so they remained until the twenty or so men who knew about the whereabouts of the body decided it was time to build a new crypt. But before Lincoln was reinterred, his coffin was opened so the group could view his body. It's said that Lincoln hadn't changed much during those twenty-two years.

Leon Hopkins, who then closed the casket and nailed it shut, thought he would be the last man to gaze upon Lincoln's face. But in 1901, Hopkins again opened the coffin lid for those who still remained in the original group. He then closed it once again for what we think was finally the final time.

Man Who Opened Lincoln's Casket Is Paid at Last

A debt incurred 52 years ago to prove that Abraham Lincoln's body had not been stolen was marked as paid today.

As part of the celebration of Lincoln's 130th birthday, Leon P. Hopkins was given a check for $22.76, representing the fee he charged for opening the casket in 1887 before a committee of 20 witnesses.

Hopkins explained he never asked for payment because he believed his task an honor and the state apparently forgot all about it.

Only Major Felix Streyckmanns, a Chicago attorney, who paid the money to Hopkins and Fleetwood R. Lindley of Springfield remain alive of the committee who viewed the body in 1887 and again in 1901 when it was interred under six feet of concrete in the memorial tomb.

Daily Journal-Gazette (Mattoon, Illinois),

Monday Evening, February 13, 1939

With all this activity, how could Lincoln find any rest? That may be why the president's ghost is often seen walking the streets of Springfield, and his home is haunted as well. Some of the paranormal experiences may be tied to Jameson Jenkins, a former slave who escaped to the Quaker town of Guilford, North Carolina. By 1838 the biracial Jenkins was living in Springfield.

A Conductor?

Lincoln Neighbor Likely Active with Underground Railroad.
By Tara McClellan McAndrew

UNTITLED DOCUMENT

"Eleven runaway slaves, belonging to citizens of St. Louis, and for which a reward of $300 each, was offered, were captured in this county yesterday, by individuals of this city," proclaimed Springfield's Jan. 17, 1850 Illinois State Register. That was the first of several articles over the next week about this so-called slave stampede in Springfield. It wasn't unusual for runaway slaves to come through Springfield, but the large number in this group must have made it stand out. Although follow-up articles in the Register and the Illinois State Journal differed in their descriptions of how large the group was and how many slaves were captured or escaped, two connected one man with the slaves—a "colored person" named "Mr. Jenkins."

The articles are contradictory and confusing: One says Jenkins betrayed the slaves to their hunters, another says he helped them escape, and still another says he was on a stage-coach the night in question. However, they could indicate that

Jenkins helped the slaves escape to Bloomington by way of stagecoach. Mr. Jenkins, it turns out, was Abraham Lincoln's neighbor.

Illinois Times, Wednesday, April 2, 2008

Though Lincoln's body most likely remains in the crypt, that doesn't keep creepy things from happening to both staff and visitors. Voices can be heard talking in places that are empty, constant pacing indicating a feverish mind, the sobs of someone in mourning echo through the house, and sudden cold spots dominate the rooms—but then it is a crypt after all. Could it be Lincoln? And why is his spirit still restlessly stirring? Prosaically, it might be that he just can't figure out where his body now rests. After all, it does make the mind reel with thoughts of coffins being moved from one place to another on such a regular basis—rather like a Midwest version of a French farce. Or, even after he passed from this earth, maybe Lincoln's mind is still consumed with an overwhelming sadness about the toll of the war, the loss of his two sons, and the division of the country he loved so much.

Abe may also haunt the Springfield home he, Mary, and their children shared, but it's Mary's ghost who seems most active there. Some see her briefly standing in a doorway before she vanishes from sight. Others are alerted to her presence by the crinoline of her long skirts rustling past in a corridor. She may have been in the parlor but she's just as suddenly gone. Her presence is so close, it's as if she's right behind, but turn your head, and Mary, again, has disappeared. But don't worry, wait long enough and she'll be almost there again.

Poet Vachel Lindsay, who was born in a house once owned by Lincoln's sister-in-law and which Lincoln had visited several times, sums up the woes and cares weighing on Lincoln and gives us another clue as to why Lincoln still roams.

This Cleveland, Columbus, and Cincinnati Railroad engine, with a portrait of Abraham Lincoln mounted on the front, was one of several used to carry Lincoln's body from Washington, D.C., to Springfield, Illinois. Photo courtesy of the Library of Congress.

Abraham Lincoln Walks at Midnight

(In Springfield, Illinois)

It is portentous, and a thing of state
That here at midnight, in our little town
A mourning figure walks, and will not rest,
Near the old court-house pacing up and down.

Or by his homestead, or in shadowed yards
He lingers where his children used to play,
Or through the market, on the well-worn stones
He stalks until the dawn-stars burn away.

A bronzed, lank man! His suit of ancient black,
A famous high top-hat and plain worn shawl
Make him the quaint great figure that men love,
The prairie-lawyer, master of us all.

He cannot sleep upon his hillside now.
He is among us:—as in times before!
And we who toss and lie awake for long
Breathe deep, and start, to see him pass the door.

His head is bowed. He thinks on men and kings.
Yea, when the sick world cries, how can he sleep?
Too many peasants fight, they know not why,
Too many homesteads in black terror weep.

The sins of all the war-lords burn his heart.
He sees the dreadnaughts scouring every main.
He carries on his shawl-wrapped shoulders now
The bitterness, the folly and the pain.

He cannot rest until a spirit-dawn
Shall come;—the shining hope of Europe free;
The league of sober folk, the Workers' Earth,
Bringing long peace to Cornland, Alp and Sea.

It breaks his heart that kings must murder still,
That all his hours of travail here for men
Seem yet in vain. And who will bring white peace
That he may sleep upon his hill again?

FIVE

Outwitting the Devil

TWO HUNDRED DOLLARS REWARD!

Ran away from the subscriber, on the 6th . . . my boy Manuel.
He is about 35 years of age, about 5 feet 7 inches high, heavy
built weighing 160 pounds. He has a shrewd expression of the
eye and has a scar on one of his thighs occasioned from a burn,
is well dress and has in his possession a figured plush
carpet-bag.

I will give a Reward of $200 for the apprehension and de-
livery of said boy at my house about ten miles from Berry's
Ferry or in the Livingston County Jail if taken in any other
state; or $50 if taken within the State of Kentucky. E. M. Duley.
Livingston Co., KY., May 9, 1860.

A man named Ned, also about thirty-five years old, was
worth $300 to his owner, according to a runaway slave ad
hanging in the Levi Coffin Interpretative Center in Fountain
City. These types of ads were not unique. For as long as there
was slavery, there were ads placed in newspapers and hung in
public places offering large amounts of money for the return
of the human beings who wanted to be free.

The very haunted Prospect Place, also known as the Trinway Mansion, in Dresden, Ohio, was a stop on the Underground Railroad. Photo courtesy of Ryan Lawrence.

The reward for Manuel is equivalent to almost $6,000 in today's money; apprehending Ned would have earned a slave catcher close to $9,000. Slave hunting was a brutal business, but a very profitable one at a time when the average wage was about $1 a day for an unskilled worker.

But slave catching had its perils, as one slave catcher learned when he came searching for bounty at Prospect Place in Dresden, Ohio. But even when the results weren't as dire, abolitionists and escaping slaves often outwitted those who came after them.

PROSPECT PLACE
DRESDEN, OHIO

Said to be the most haunted house in Ohio, the stately and costly Prospect Place, also known as the Trinway Mansion, was completed in 1856 as the home of abolitionist George W. Adams and his second wife, Mary, and it became a stop on the Underground Railroad.

George W. and his brother Edward were the sons of George B. Adams, a Revolutionary War veteran who during his time fighting for his country had fully embraced the concept of all men being equal. Despite inheriting his father's plantation—land encompassing some five hundred acres— the senior Adams decided to move to Ohio, which in 1803 joined the Union and was a free state, in part because of his unpopular antislavery views.

When their father died, leaving them 150 acres of fertile Virginia land, the two brothers decided to build a gristmill on the Ohio-Erie Canal. The water from the canal powered the mill's wheel, turning grain into flour, which could then be shipped directly to such ports as New Orleans.

"This increased the number of ways the Adams brothers had to get their flour to market," writes George J. Adams. "The mill was built and became a huge success. George and Edward both married and had families. The brothers built identical homes for a cost of $40,000 each. They were magnificent and large homes."

They must have been magnificent indeed, as $40,000 in the mid-1800s is equivalent to about $1.2 million today. Married with five children, George W. was successful in both business and politics, winning a seat to the Ohio General Assembly. But when his wife Clarissa died giving birth to another George (who would also pass away in a few months), Adams was devastated. After meeting and successfully courting Mary Jane Robinson (she would give him another two children), Adams didn't want to remain in the home he'd shared with Clarissa.

"He decided he could no longer live in the house 'of bad memories' and would build for his new wife a 'fairy tale castle' in which they could live happily ever after," his son wrote in "Prospect Place: The George Willison Adams Mansion."

The ground was broken for the mansion and hundreds of laborers were hired. The family watched from the little wooden house as a great brick edifice arose from the fields on the knoll to the north. Three stories it rose, a two story wing, almost another house unto itself for the servants grew to the north and a cupola crowned the top. Glowing copper panels formed the roof and brightly colored paint trimmed the ornate gingerbread porticoes. Sooner than anyone thought possible the house was complete. It stood glowing in the summer sun of 1856, a testimony in brick to the community and family that made it happen.

The night before the family was to move in, the house caught fire and burned to the ground. A bucket brigade arrived too late and could not get near the inferno for the heat. Some people said an elderly Native American woman simply called "Satan" had burned the house because it sat atop the burial place of her people, the Shawnee. The more likely explanation is that of a bricklayer on the project named George Blackburn. He was a notorious character who, when he was not robbing and plundering, worked as a bricklayer in the Dresden area. He supposedly bragged in a drunken stupor to someone in Dresden of having burned the mansion in order to generate more work for himself. George W. Adams heard of this and promptly had Mr. Blackburn arrested and sent to the Columbus Penitentiary. Blackburn had helped build the prison and was able to escape soon thereafter. He returned to Muskingum County where he met his end through the splitting axe of a farmer he attempted to rob in the area of what is now Ellis Dam. Prospect Place, the name George Adams gave his mansion as it was to be the prospect of a better future, was immediately rebuilt.

Maybe there was some truth as to the spot being a Shawnee burial ground, but Prospect Place, which still stands and is now owned once again by a member of the Adams family, does indeed seem to be filled with ghosts, each representing different eras. One haunt is Anna Adams-Cox, the eldest daughter of George and Clarissa Adams and the wife of W. E. Cox. The couple lived at Prospect Place after the death of her father, or at least they did until W. E. disappeared one day after saying he was going to Zanesville on business. With her husband gone, the family fortunes depleted, and the house falling to ruin, Anna took her trials and tribulations to the grave with her and her restless spirit is part of the repertoire of ghostly inhabitants.

As for her husband, his disappearance was never solved but clues can be found in various news accounts.

A Missing Man

W. E. Cox, who owns large landed interests near Trinway, this county, is missing and it is rumored that he had $1,800 with him. He advertised a sale to take place at his home November 16, but as he was not there it was postponed. He was seen Friday evening, November 15, at the Chittenden Hotel, Columbus and leaving there walked south on High Street. Neither his wife nor his friends know anything of him since that date.

Daily Herald (Delphos, Ohio), Thursday, November 28, 1895

Very Common Occurrence

W. E. Cox of Zanesville came here with $800 in his pocket about two weeks ago, since which time no trace of him can be found.

Ohio Democrat (Logan, Ohio), Saturday, November 30, 1895

Cox Had Better Come Back

At Zanesville Judge Munson, of the common pleas court, has granted judgements in the following cases: John W. Cassingham against William E. Cox for $157.70 in default. Mr. Cassingham also asked to be relieved of all liability as

Mr. Cox's surety on an injunction bond of $7000. A judgement by default for $3500 was taken in behalf of the plaintiff and an order of sale was granted in both cases. W. E. is the defendant in another case in which W. L. Robinson, of this county, is plaintiff. A judgement for $77,000 was taken in this case and the sheriff was ordered to sell the real estate upon which the lien was granted.

Democratic Standard (Coshocton, Ohio), Friday,
February 7, 1896

A barn and all its contents, including 3000 bushels of wheat belonging to W. E. Cox of Dresden was destroyed by fire last Saturday night. Loss $6000; insurance $4000. Supposed to be incendiary.

Coshocton Tribune (Coshocton, Ohio), Friday, August 27, 1886

Is Will Cox Dead?

That is the question agitating the public today—or if not dead what has become of him? The mysterious disappearance of Mr. William E. Cox, whose country residence, Prospect Place, located between Dresden and Trinway is the most palatial in the county, has been the theme of conversation in this community for the past week. While it was known last week that he had disappeared and no trace of him could be found, although a detective had been put on his trail, yet it was hoped and thought he would turn up and through respect for the feelings of his family and connections this paper refrained from mentioning the matter in any respect.

But Mr. Cox is gone as completely as if the very earth had opened up and swallowed him and in spite of every effort made to get some trace of him by his family, his legal advisors and his friends none can be had. Mr. Cox left home on Friday, November 15, just before noon, informing his family that he

The Fox Valley Ghost Hunters, a paranormal investigation group, found a lot of activity at the very haunted Prospect Place. Shown here are members of the team. Photo courtesy of Craig Nehring, Fox Valley Ghost Hunters.

was going to Zanesville on business, and that as he was in a hurry he would not stop for dinner.

When he arrived at Trinway he spoke to Henry Park and said he wished he had someone to do an errand for him in Zanesville as he had some business in Columbus and it would put him out very much if he did not go to attend to it. Mr. Park said his wife was on the C & M.V. train which would soon start for Zanesville, and she could attend to Mr. Cox's errand, and the latter gentleman gave Mr. Park $255, and told him to have Mrs. Park pay it to A. E. Starr & Co., on his (Cox's) account. He then took the Panhandle train for Columbus.

http://www.gwacenter.org/disappearance
_of_william_cox.htm

W. E. Cox Located

Seen on the streets of San Francisco by Miss Jennie Adams, who formerly resided here. Mrs. W. E. Cox has received a letter from Jennie Adams, daughter of the late Samuel Adams and who was born and for the greater part of her life resided in

Dresden, in which she states that she met Mr. Cox a few days ago upon the streets of San Francisco, California, in company with a strange gentleman.

Having been absent from Dresden several years and having been intimately acquainted with Mr. Cox she was naturally very much pleased at seeing him and advanced towards him calling his name and asking a question about his folks, etc., almost in the same breath. He seemed annoyed, did not speak a word to her and hastily swept past her. She started after him and seeing her following he entered a cigar store.

She thinking perhaps he did not recognize her followed him in but he passed on into a side way and hid from her. She had no knowledge of his disappearance here and, being an old friend of his wife's, wrote to Mrs. Cox telling about Will's strange action. It was undoubtedly Mr. Cox as it seems impossible that she could be mistaken and then his actions almost verify his identity.

A peculiar and interesting matter has developed in connection with the disappearance of Mr. Cox. On November 8 he was a guest at Schrader's hotel in Columbus and had with him a friend whom he refused to register and he and the clerk had a few warm words over the affair. A good description has been obtained of this man from Schrader's clerk and the peculiar and perhaps significant part of it comes when the strange man who was seen with Mr. Cox in San Francisco by Miss Adams, and whom she minutely describes, tallies to a dot with the description of the person furnished by Schrader's clerk.

Mrs. Cox feels perfectly satisfied that Miss Adams could make no mistake and that the man she saw in California is none other than her husband, W. E. Cox. Why he is there no one but himself knows at present but perhaps later developments may sometime reveal his object for his, to say the least, strange and unnatural actions.

http://www.gwacenter.org/disappearance
_of_william_cox.htm

Although George J. Adams writes that Cox never returned to Prospect Place during his real life, his ghost is also said to walk the grounds and home.

Even before Anna died, the mansion had already fallen into disrepair, says Jeffrey Cole, one of the trustees of the nonprofit G. W. Adams Educational Center, which was created to help preserve and restore the home and educational outreach opportunities.

"With the family financial fortunes having been lost in the decades preceding her death, the mansion was ultimately willed to other descendants, none of whom had much interest in it," says Cole. "By the 1960s and 70s, the house had essentially been abandoned and broken into numerous times. The vandalism and destruction was simply horrendous. Coupled with decades of time and literally no maintenance the mansion was in terrible condition."

In a curious twist of fate, the mansion, which had been sold, is now again in the possession of Jeffrey George Adams, the great-great-grandson of George W. and, with the support of the Longaberger family (of the Longaberger basket fame), the ultimate goal is to turn Prospect Place into a Heritage Tourism destination site.

How the ghosts might feel about the intrusion of tourists is not known. Prospect Place is also said to be haunted by a little girl who fell to her death from her upstairs bedroom window on a winter night. As the ground was too frozen to dig her grave, her body instead was stored in the basement until spring. Her grief stricken mother stayed by her daughter's side during those cold, sad months, ultimately developing pneumonia and perishing as well. Both haunt Prospect Place, the little girl wandering the house, sometimes seen on the stairs or in her upstairs room. From the basement come the sounds of her cries. Her mother can be found in the basement where she kept her long and fatal vigil as well as in her daughter's room.

The ghost of an escaped slave who was hidden in the basement remains there as well; his or her job is to tend to the body of the little girl.

"Almost all of the ghosts we encountered there were nice," says Craig Nehring, founder of the Fox Valley Ghost Hunters (FVGH) who did a paranormal investigation at Prospect Place.

FVGH's interactions with Prospect Place's spectral inhabitants occurred mostly in the basement and included being touched, a little bed bouncing on which a team member rested, and the sounds of voices and screams.

Nehring attributes this activity to the death of the little girl and her body being kept there through the winter.

The team's investigation lasted for two nights, and, in their report, they note that on the first night while in the basement their paranormal experiences included "some shadows pop right up in front of us and some of the investigators had someone grab their shoulder or run a hand over their head. We did some audio sessions to try to get EVP and our founder Craig yelled Marco five times and got Polo back three of the five times he yelled it and once we heard something yell Polo.

"The second day we all played some football and waited for night to set in so we could investigate some more," the report continues. "We sat around, cooked some food, and we set up cameras and got everything going for the night. We were greeted with some footsteps up in the room by the cross and found some really cold spots. We lucked out this time and no girls screamed. Later in the morning when we went to bed something shut off our cameras and we checked the footage but can't explain why they went off. One of the investigators said someone was kicking his mattress and he was too tired to get up and eventually it stopped."

Nehring describes the hauntings at Prospect Place as almost continuous.

"The ghosts are there pretty much all the time," he says. "It's just whether they want to be seen."

The only malevolent ghost said to haunt Prospect Place belongs to a brutal slave catcher who ventured onto the property hunting for runaways. The story of the Bounty Hunter is a significant part of Prospect Place's oral history, says Cole, noting it's one that's been handed down through the generations, though no historic documentation exists. But then again, given that the tale is about vigilante justice, none of the participants were likely to have recorded their crime.

"The legend goes that a bounty hunter, under the auspices of the Fugitive Slave Act, came to Prospect Place in pursuit of runaway slaves," says Cole. "Whether he was in hot pursuit of a band of runaways or following a lead that Prospect Place was a safe house is unknown. When he arrived seeking to search the mansion, he was confronted with an armed and less than cooperative G. W. Adams, who forbade him access to his home, ultimately chasing him off. As all good legends and mysteries go, things get murky. Did Mr. Adams send his hired hands after the bounty hunter or did his friends and neighbors act on their own accord? Your guess is as good as mine. Of course, it's reasonable to assume that a bounty hunter who was prevented from collecting on his quarry or searching a suspected safe house could likely find sympathetic locals or other bounty hunters and return causing a major scandal, panic, and/or a disruption to peaceful rural life."

Did George W. know? Again there's no documentation. But Cole has his own theory.

"Personally and unofficially, I tend to think that Mr. Adams probably had a pretty good idea of what was going on at his property and inside his barn," he says. "As a founding father of the region with significant real and financial holdings, he had a lot at stake and a lot to potentially lose if his safe house and clandestine activities were discovered. Again, personally and unofficially speaking I think it was with a wink and a nod. He closed the door and went to bed. This being said, I can also report that evidence, such as human remains, have never been found or excavated from the barn or its adjacent grounds. I should also report that in my years of association with Prospect Place, the barn and adjacent grounds have never been archaeologically surveyed or scrutinized. In short, if there's a body there, we haven't found it yet."

WESTFIELD, INDIANA

It took cunning and courage to outfox slave hunters and owners intent on bringing their "property" back to the Confederate states. But many of the people of Westfield, a town in central Indiana settled by Quakers in 1834 with the goal of making it a stop on the Underground Railroad, had the necessary qualities to do just that.

Nathan Hunt was an abolitionist who pretended to help a slave hunter searching for George Hoard, who, with his wife and child, had come to Westfield via the UGRR. When the bounty hunter recognized the Hoard child, he seized him. Defending the child, Hunt brandished a thick stick and, threatening to strike the slave catcher said, "Thee put that child down, it is none of thine." The slave catcher, measuring his odds, gave in, releasing the child and leaving the family in safety.

Michael Kobrowski and his wife Nicole own Indiana Ghost Walks and Tours in Westfield, which offers such ghostly historic tours as the Haunted Underground Railroad Walking Tour. Kobrowski tells the story of Singleton Vaughn, who laid claim to John and Louann Rhodes and their family. Armed with a warrant for their capture from a judge in Strawtown and—as a backup to those pieces of paper—loaded shotguns, Vaughn arrived with five rough-looking men in Westfield in 1844. The Rhodeses had settled near town in 1839 after fleeing a farm in Missouri and, while the community was welcoming, John Rhodes, fearful of slave catchers, built his log cabin minus windows and with just one very solid door. Picking up an axe at the sound of armed men and standing by the door with his family behind him, Rhodes shut the stout door and stood ready as the men approached.

What happened next is described by David Heighway in "The Law in Black and White."

When the slavecatchers broke the door down, John re-barricaded it with furniture. When they tore down the chimney, Louann was on the other side with hot coals and a large stick of firewood. So a standoff ensued, while John and Louann shouted for help from the neighbors, making as much noise as possible. One version of the story says that the neighbors heard the shouting and came running.

Court records indicate that John surrendered when he saw his family threatened by the guns, but asked to be taken to a neighbor's house to collect a fifty-dollar debt. Vaughn agreed since, as the slave owner, it was actually his money since slaves couldn't own property. But it was a clever ploy. There was no debt and the neighbor, an Underground Railroad operator, immediately challenged Vaughn's rights to the family. As they talked, more and more people arrived at the scene. Vaughn, angry and feeling justified in retrieving his property, threatened anyone who tried to intervene but finally was convinced to go before a judge to determine the legitimacy of his claim. At that point Vaughn had little choice; even though he and his men were armed, they were outnumbered and besides, it would be murder to shoot into the crowd. The

Rhodes family climbed into a wagon, ostensibly to be driven to the judge's. Their wagon proceeded south but when they reached the intersection of two roads, now Highways 38 and 31, the crowd following them had increased in number to around 150 people, most of whom were hostile toward Vaughn and his men. At the intersection, a fight broke out. The majority of the crowd wanted to go to Westfield to find a judge. Vaughn, knowing it was a nest of abolitionists, insisted on Noblesville. Among the disagreement and confusion of the large crowd, as a result, a standoff ensued.

A man named Daniel Jones leapt into the wagon seat, told the slave-catchers to shoot if they dared, and whipped the horses toward Westfield. Momentarily stunned before being able to spring into action, the slave-catchers then found themselves blocked from following right away and hence the Rhodes family made it to Westfield ahead of them.

Finally making it to Westfield, the slave hunters discovered they were too late; the Rhodes family had escaped at some point during the ride.

There's another variation to the story. This one tells of the Rhodes, having been captured, being driven out of town when either Rhodes or one of the crowd told Vaughn he owed the ex-slave money and he should stop by and get it. Vaughn agreed and once arriving at the home was invited to stay for breakfast. When finished eating, the slave hunters boarded their wagon, but before they could be on their way, a large party of abolitionists arrived.

"In the ensuing fight, two teenagers jumped aboard the wagon and rode off with the Rhodes, and when the slave hunters caught up with them later, the Rhodes family was gone," says Kobrowski.

But it wasn't over yet. Aggrieved, Vaughn took his case to court believing he had the law on his side.

A Slave Case
Indiana State Sentinel, **November 28, 1844**

Vaughn's premise was that the crowd didn't have the right to interfere with his attempt to retake his property. He didn't win his case in court in part because the laws of another state didn't make the resident of the state they were living a slave and because Missouri, where the Rhodes came from, was not an original state. Plus, the Rhodes family had lived in Illinois for a while, another free state. Vaughn tried suing again the following year but with no luck.

In six years, with the passage of the 1850 Fugitive Slave Law, Vaughn would have had much better luck as the law made it easier to reclaim slaves with the following provisions:

- Federal jurisdiction over fugitive slaves.
- Creation of paid posse to assist in capture of escaped slaves.
- Increased penalties for anyone assisting an escaped slave (fine of $1,000 and/or imprisonment for six months plus damages to slave owner).
- Financial incentives to federal commissioners—a bounty of $10 paid for each returned slave—only $5 if slave released.

A Slave Hunter Outwitted

Reminiscences of Levi Coffin, the Reputed President of the Underground Railroad.

> The story that I am about to relate may, in some of its particulars, seem improbable or even impossible, to any reader not acquainted with the workings of the southern division of the Underground Railroad. That two young slave girls could successfully make their escape from a Southern State and travel hundreds of miles, hiding in the day, in thickets and other

secluded places, and traveling at night, crossing rivers and swamps, and passing undiscovered through settlements, appears more like a story of romance than one of sober reality.

Taken in by residents of Cabin Creek, a free black settlement near Fountain City, two young girls had their freedom threatened again when their owner learned where they were living. Determined to reclaim them but hearing that the residents of Cabin Creek banded together to protect fugitives, he hired "roughs" from nearby towns, and they began to ride toward the settlement. A young boy, knowing of their approach, jumped on a horse and began riding to summon help. The slave hunters fired at him, grazing his arm, but he got away.

The grandfather of the young girls was away, but the grandmother seized a corn cutter and placed herself in the only door of the cabin, declaring she would cut in two the first man who tried to enter. The boy's alarm had attracted a crowd, which grew to more than two hundred, blacks and whites, including those who were both proslavery and antislavery. Joining his mother in the doorway, the girls' uncle and several other sturdy blacks blocked the way.

The uncle asked to see the writ and then debated with the slave master about its legality and whether he was truly the owner of the girls. As they talked, several people from the Cabin Creek community entered and left the cabin, including the girls, who were dressed in boys' clothing and wore large slouched hats. Riding away on fleet horses, they made the twenty-mile journey to Coffin's home, where they arrived tired and hungry and were put to bed.

We did not apprehend any danger that night, as we supposed a vigorous search would be made at Cabin Creek and neighboring settlements, and that our town would not be searched till the hunt in the other localities had been prosecuted and proved fruitless.

The Levi Coffin home in Fountain City. It's estimated that Levi and his wife, Catharine, helped two thousand men, women, and children escape from slavery. Photo courtesy of Jane Simon Ammeson.

The next day, Coffin received a message that members of the posse were on their way to Fountain City. He went home to tell his wife and then returned to the store, noting that "she was used to such business and was not long in devising a plan."

And so Aunt Katy did. She hid the girls between the straw tick and feather tick (two mattresses made up of bedding material), smoothed the quilt, and placed pillows on the bed. But the girls were so excited and amused, and the remembrance of how they outwitted the slave owners, their ride dressed in boys' clothes, and all that had happened set them giggling. So Katy had to separate the girls, placing them in different beds. But, in the end, it didn't matter, as Coffin recounts in his book.

> If the searchers attempted to enter our house, she was to rattle the large dinner bell violently, and at this signal the neighbors would rush in, and I would get the proper officers and have the

Tricks of the trade for hiding and transporting runaway slaves include a wagon with a hidden compartment, such as the one in the barn on the Coffin property. Photo courtesy of Jane Simon Ammeson.

negro hunters arrested for attempting to enter my house without legal authority.

But these proceedings were not necessary. The hunters did not have courage enough to enter my house, though they knew it was a depot of the Underground Railroad. Hearing that threats were made against them in the village, they left without giving us any trouble.

We kept the girls very secluded for several weeks until the master had given up the search, and gone home. Then having other fugitives to forward to the North, we sent them altogether via the Greenville and Sandusky route to Canada, where they arrived in safety.

SIX

Ghostly Overload

I ALWAYS ASSUMED ghosts were site specific. But as I learned from Hal Yeagy, owner of the Slippery Noodle Inn, an 1850 hotel, restaurant, and Underground Railroad stop in Indianapolis, ghosts can move around as their old haunts are torn down and they need another familiar setting and nearby place to stay.

But it gets even more complicated than that.

Ghost-producing events—think murders, suicides, grisly accidents, and untimely deaths—multiply as the years go by. More time, more bad things, particularly in places like hotels and bars.

If during the decades a ghost or two result from such events, suddenly there's a plethora of apparitions, each with its own agenda and needs, floating around. Who are they and why are they here are questions confronting ghost hunters and those who have to interact with them on a regular basis, such as property owners. After all, ghosts don't wear name tags and hand out their bios when they come a-haunting.

Often it's a guess as to who is a hanger-on from the Underground Railroad days and who became ghostly due to, say, a cholera epidemic, an overdose of chloroform, a jealous

Craig Nehring of the Fox Valley Ghost Hunters captured the image of a Civil War–era soldier when doing an investigation at the Iola Mill in Iola, Wisconsin. Photo courtesy of Tom and Melody Fucik.

lover, or a dastardly murder plot. So just knowing that a property was the site of the UGRR and is also haunted doesn't always guarantee we'll know the entire story of why the ghosts are there, but in this chapter we try our best.

IOLA MILL
IOLA, WISCONSIN

"I captured him with a thermal camera," says Craig Nehring, a member of the Fox Valley Ghost Hunters (FVGH), talking about the image of a Civil War soldier he took at the Millstone of Iola Mill. "We don't know a lot about him, but when I got the picture, he was standing there behind a group of people. It was interesting because they found the Civil War hat he was wearing downstairs in the area where they had all this old stuff."

Now owned by Tom and Melody Fucik and called the Millstone of Iola Mill, the gristmill was developed around

Now a restaurant called the Millstone of Iola Mill, the haunted grain mill has been part of the community since the 1850s. This is Iola Mill as it looked in 1880. Photo courtesy of Tom and Melody Fucik.

1854, when Silas Miller dammed the river to harness power to run both grist and saw mills. The ownership of the mills quickly passed through several hands, until 1857, when Henry Wipf, a Swiss immigrant, and his two sons took over a majority of the mill and purchased it completely, according to Tom Fucik, in 1863.

Jacob and Conrad fought in the Civil War (Fucik says they have a couple of muskets that most likely belonged to them) and started families when they returned home. Conrad had two children, and Jacob just one son, John Edwin Wipf, who was killed in a mill accident in 1884— his neck snapped by one of the big belts that turned the apparatus.

"The Wipf family owned the mill for about a century," says Fucik. "Conrad's son, Fred, took it over, and Fred's son, Freddie, was the last member of the family to own the mill."

By 1963, when Freddie Wipf sold the gristmill, the old sawmill built by his ancestors had long ago been torn. The property went through a series of owners, including Bob and Stella Strand, who turned the mill into a local history museum. When the Fuciks bought it in 1996, they closed the museum and undertook an extensive restoration of the mill and its grounds, opening a restaurant and hosting live music and special events. Now on the National Register of Historic Places, the mill has its share of ghost stories and hauntings.

"I haven't seen it but I have evidence of the inexplicable," says Tom. "In the spot where I assume that John Edwin was killed, whenever we go in there, there's a pile of dust and grain. It's always just in that one spot and it's a hundred times more than anyone would expect. When that happens we go upstairs to check to see if there's a reason for it being there. But there just isn't anything there that tells us how it got there."

Strange happenings occur with the electricity as well.

"One winter when we were closed and the place was shut up tight, I was the only one there and a live wire was cut in three places," he says. "These kinds of things always happen in the same places."

Unlike her husband, Melody Fucik has seen an apparition. In what she calls "my ghost story," she recounts walking along the lake one night with Mikey, the family dog. Normally easygoing and obedient, Mikey suddenly ran in front of her and stopped, refusing to let her walk any farther. For a reason she still doesn't understand, Melody felt compelled to look up at the mill. There in the third-floor window she could see a figure looking out at her. Because her husband was home and she knew the mill was locked and empty, Melody quickly realized the figure was that of someone from the mill's past.

"Mikey knew it was there too," says Melody, who joined in when the Fox Valley Ghost Hunters did their investigation.

"When Fox Valley came, they looked at the first floor and used all their equipment but didn't get anything," recalls Tom. "They got a little something on the second floor and more on the third floor. It was interesting. They didn't get any response when they asked 'Are you John Edwin,' the son who was killed. There was no response when they asked 'Are you Fred?' But when they said 'Are you Freddie,' everything lit up."

Here Fucik stops, thinking about Freddie Wipf, who sold the mill in 1963.

"It had to be heart-wrenching for Freddie to sell it, after four generations of family owning it."

FVGH team members also detected an energy source next to Melody, which they thought might be Mikey, the beloved family dog who had died recently. Melody believes that as well.

As for the image of the Civil War soldier, the Fuciks saw the photo Nehring took but they really don't know who the man could be, even though, among the many artifacts left from when the mill was a museum, Nehring found the Civil War hat that matched the one the ghost was wearing.

Like other places with a long history, there's certainly an abundance of ghostly characters, including John Edwin, Mikey the dog, and the Civil War soldier. Another addition could be Amelia Wipf, who was just nineteen when she gave birth to John Edwin, her only child. A grieving mother just might decide to remain near the site where her son met his tragic death. But it's the Civil War ghost that is most mysterious. Sure, both Connor and Jacob went off to fight in the war, but they returned, healthy and strong. Though there wasn't much UGRR activity in this part of Wisconsin, maybe a few

Haunted by the ghosts of runaway slaves, McCourtie Park in Somerset, Michigan, was one of Michigan's Underground Railroad routes, and is said to be haunted by other spirits as well. The most common sighting is the ghost of a woman wearing blue, but gangsters who used to make the run between Detroit and Chicago during Prohibition are said to roam here as well. The park itself has a ghostly atmosphere. It took two artists ten years to create the *faux bois* (imitation wood) structures, including seventeen bridges, for owner and cement magnate William McCourtie. Photo courtesy of Jane Simon Ammeson.

runaway slaves came through here on their way to Canada. Did one or two remain to haunt the mill?

Nehring says he and his team are looking forward to conducting another investigation. Hopefully he'll find out then.

McCOURTIE PARK
SOMERSET, MICHIGAN

A Native American trading route, the Old Sauk Trail connected Chicago to Detroit and was also one of Michigan's Underground Railroad routes running through the northern

Though from a distance the bridges and stunted trees in McCourtie Park look like wood, they are really sculpted out of concrete in an almost forgotten folk style known as *el trabejo rustico*, which translates to "rustic work." Photo courtesy of Jane Simon Ammeson.

edge of Indiana and up into Michigan, merging near Adrian with another of the state's UGRR trails—that bringing slaves from Toledo, Ohio. Today, the Old Sauk Trail is US 12, a heritage trail that meanders through the small towns and villages of the southernmost part of Michigan. Along the way, tucked almost out of sight in the small town of Somerset, is McCourtie Park.

Though the park, once part of the estate of W. H. L. McCourtie, wasn't here when the runaway slaves followed the Sauk Trail toward Detroit, the area, sparsely populated with a creek for fresh water and wooded glens for resting undiscovered, would have made a good stopping point. Besides, this area of Michigan, settled by those from Europe who had come to America to escape religious persecution, had Northern sensibilities toward slavery.

Most agree that McCourtie Park is haunted, and there are more ghosts than just Native Americans and runaway slaves still present here. Al Capone supposedly visited, his gangsters making the run from Chicago to Detroit.

McCourtie, the millionaire owner of the Trinity Portland Cement Company, had a fondness for both concrete and whimsy, and his estate, known as Aiden Lair, was the perfect place to create a fantastical garden. Today, his home is gone but the park remains—a fairy-tale place where nature has been carved out of cement.

Here cement chimneys created to look like tree trunks rise out of a rathskeller built into the side of a hill where McCourtie (known as Herb to his friends) played poker with such Detroit bigwigs as auto baron Henry Ford. Local lore says that tunnels used to run underground here, perfect for bootleggers to smuggle in liquor for those all-night poker games. Seventeen folk-art-style bridges cross the meandering stream on the forty-two-acre property.

These unique sculptures, called *el trabejo rustico*, Spanish for "rustic work," were created by Mexican artisans Dionicio Rodriquez and Ralph Corona of Texas (McCourtie had made it big as a Texas oil man before returning home to Somerset). Also known by the French term, *faux bois*, or "fake wood," the artwork involves a complex process of shaping, molding, staining, and adding texture to the concrete so that it looks amazingly real. McCourtie admired this early to mid-twentieth-century folk art, now very seldom used. Each bridge is uniquely fashioned as the cross the waterways and lead into wooded glades. One bridge, surely designed for gnomes, has the look of a thatched cottage, albeit a cement one; another resembles an old-fashioned swinging bridge, the cement scored in a way to look like ropes and wood; planked seats, also fashioned out of cement, invite visitors to stop halfway across and rest.

Weeping willows crowd the sides of the stream, dripping long, feathery branches on the waters. Benches and elaborate birdhouses, including several tall purple martin homes capable of sheltering more than two hundred birds, are half hidden in the woods.

It's the perfect place for a ghost and indeed, it's here that the Lady in Blue, a svelte woman dressed in a blue gown, moves quietly across one of the bridges.

"I've never seen the Lady in Blue," says John Koch, who grew up in the area and as a kid joined his friends in the park. "But I know people who have. They say she wears a period dress like from the 1930s and that it's repetitive what she does—she goes from point A to point B and then she disappears. People wonder why she does that. My theory is something happened to her there or that it was a place that has a nice memory for her. The story was that the rathskeller was a speakeasy. We know for a fact that US 12 was a thoroughfare for people like Al Capone."

The repetitive activity of the Lady in Blue is what Craig Nehring of the Fox Valley Ghost Hunters describes as a residual haunting, or restligeist, a ghost that is just repeating or replaying a certain point in time. Often that's linked to a traumatic or life-altering event, which can present itself in either auditory or visual phenomena. In these cases, the spiritual entity might not be aware of the living who are around them and they don't typically respond or react to the living either.

Koch, who is a member of the McCourtie Park Facebook group, says that when he was growing up he and his friends heard rumors that there were tunnels underground that might connect to the cement plant in Cement City.

"We used to sneak over there even though we weren't supposed to be there," he says. "We'd be snooping around trying to find the tunnels. When you get really close to the building, you have this really weird feeling, not that someone is watching you but that that you just shouldn't be there, that there was something going on. It's really hard to explain but you just really feel it."

Koch and his friends never did find the tunnels and he doesn't know, if they do exist, what they were used for. Some stories have them being used by runaway slaves and later by bootleggers. He hypothesizes that the tunnels could really have been ditches running through farmland where slaves, crouching low, could make their way toward Detroit without being seen.

As for the Lady in Blue? Her outfit puts her more with the speakeasy crowd. Maybe she drowned in one of the park's cement ponds or maybe she was killed by a jealous lover.

That would surprise Koch, who has never heard of a murder in the park or on the grounds of the McCourtie mansion. Like the ghosts of the Underground Railroad and those mysterious tunnels, the Lady in Blue remains a mystery.

THE ROCKPORT INN
ROCKPORT, INDIANA

Children running up and down the hallway rattling door knobs and trying to peek into rooms, the piano playing on the first floor though no one is nearby, and the tall man in a dark coat standing by the bed of a sleeping patron are all manifestations of the spirits said to haunt the Rockport Inn, a stop on the Underground Railroad. Its location near the Ohio River made it the perfect spot for runaway slaves escaping from Kentucky and points farther south.

It was built in 1850 as a private home, one of the first in the area to have real glass windows. The inn's owner, Jane Stevenson, began to take in boarders after the death of her husband. Changing hands over the years, around the turn of the last century the home was owned by Sally and Harry Poole, who lived on the property and ran it under the name Cottage Hotel.

The hotel seems to have prospered but the Pooles had issues.

James Harry Poole and Sally Shaw married the first time in December of 1893 and divorced on February 9, 1906.

SALLIE POOLE VS. JAMES H. POOLE

SPENCER COUNTY CIVIL ORDER BOOK

The defendant is by the court permitted to visit said children on each week every Saturday from [...] o'clock a.m. to six o'clock p.m. until the further order of this Court providing that he abstain from the use of intoxicating liquor while visiting said children and shall be sober at the time of making such visits.

But the divorce didn't last long and just two months later the couple remarried in May. The handwritten divorce decree above indicates alcohol playing a major part in the dissolution of the marriage but whether Harry won Sally back by sobering up isn't known.

Sally owned the hotel for forty years, but Harry didn't stay in the game as long and he exited in a very dramatic way.

A Sad Affair

The city was startled Sunday morning about 10 o'clock when it was learned that Harry Poole had taken his life in the presence of his family by firing a bullet into right temple, dying almost instantly.

Mr. Poole had been in poor health for several years, having suffered a paralytic stroke about six years ago and it is thought that his ill health and the fact that a sister, Mrs. Belle Sallee, and a brother, Arthur Poole, had died within the last few weeks was more than he could stand. Just before he did the

The Rockport Inn, built circa 1850, is situated on the Ohio River and was a stop on the Underground Railroad. Hauntings include a piano playing when no one is there, footsteps on the stairs, ghosts in the dining room, and several apparitions, one of whom is a woman in a long nineteenth-century dress. Photo courtesy of William Miller, founder of Southern Indiana Paranormal Investigators.

rash act his daughter, Mrs. Armorel Kerstein, asked him if he did not feel well. He said: "No, I am never well; I am always sick." She suggested that he lie down and he did so. After lying for a few moments he reached under his pillow, secured the gun and before anyone could interfere, fired the fatal shot.

Rockport Journal, Friday, April 12, 1929

But though he physically left this earth, Harry's ghost is commonly seen, and he isn't alone. Among the other ghostly residents of the Rockport Inn is the spirit of a runaway slave.

"On the edges of the basement, there's a spot where there was a chimney," says Stacey Schulte, who bought the Rockport Inn sixteen years ago. "It goes up to the first level and that's where they hid people when it was a stop on the Underground Railroad."

As for ghosts, count Schulte as an unbeliever, though that's beginning to change since buying the inn.

"I never believed in any of that, I would have told them they're crazy, insane," she says about people who thought the place was haunted.

That was until one day when Schulte and her daughter, who was about three at the time, were making cookies.

"She came in from the dining room to help and said 'mommy, the ghosties are here,'" recalls Schulte. "I had only heard of one ghost haunting this place so I said 'are they a boy or a girl?' And she said a boy and a girl."

The ghost story Schulte was most familiar with up until that point was that of Harry Poole.

"That's who a lot of people see and they usually see him upstairs looking out of the window," says Schulte, who has never run into Harry.

The ghosts make noises but overall seem friendly—if somewhat inclined to playing pranks. But then, haunting forever may get a little tedious, so some levity can be excused.

"Guests have complained about the door knobs rattling and the piano playing late at night," she says. "We've had guests say someone or something touched them. Lots of guests say the doors open and shut, but nobody came in. Some say ghosts circle their bed at night when they're sleeping. Pictures fall off walls. We've had baskets on the shelves in the kitchen fall down even though there's no one around. They said ghosts don't like it when you change things but we're not really changing things, we want to keep the inn the way it is."

She also mentions that her ex-husband heard footsteps when no one else was at the inn.

There were other untimely deaths as well.

Girl Suicides at Rockport

The body of 19-year-old Goldie Hiles was found in her room in the Cottage hotel at 11 o'clock Wednesday, a chloroform bottle beside her.

She had gone to her room Tuesday and after repeated attempts to awaken her Wednesday morning her door was forced open.

She came here for the fair with a shooting gallery partner and it is said she is the daughter of well-to-do parents in Jacksonville, Illinois. The body will be held forward for them.

Evansville Press, Thursday, August 24, 1911

Goldie Evelyn Hiles . . . who was working for W. J. Enthofen, a concession man on the Rockport fairgrounds, committed suicide by the chloroform route Tuesday night at the Cottage Hotel in this city. Enthofen . . . has a string of shooting galleries. The unfortunate girl's brother at Jacksonville, Illinois, has been notified. Coroner A. J. Maslowsky telephoned that he would be down on the night train. In the meantime, the body lies in the room, untouched and undisturbed.

The girl came in from the fairgrounds last night about 7:30 and went to her room. She did not get up this morning and about noon Enthofen sent in a boy to tell her to come to the fairgrounds at once. Miss Anna Abshire, the landlady, knocked on the door but got no response. Going around to the side window she saw the girl lying on the bed. She sent the boy back after Enthofen and summoned Dr. O. Baumgaertner who came and gained entrance to the room by the window. He found the body lying on the bed nude and life had been gone for a number of hours. Around the head and covering the mouth and nose was a towel. It is supposed that a bottle of chloroform was in the towel. She was lying on her side with her face partially buried between two pillows. Decomposition had already set in.

Miss Hiles became acquainted with Enthofen last spring while he was running a picture show in Jacksonville. She is an attractive looking girl and had a large suit of dark red hair. Enthofen says he knows of no cause for the act.

Tribune (Seymour, Indiana), Saturday, August 26, 1911

But the story of Goldie Hiles and William Enthofen gets somewhat more complicated. One newspaper reported that she had eloped to Rockport (supposedly with him) and then, regretting her rash decision, committed suicide.

Then there's this strange story which took place about a year before her death.

Burned with Acid:
Black Hand Letters May Furnish Clue to Party Who Threw It.

Illinois Girl Was the Victim.
Jacksonville Beauty Fired Twice at Unknown Party—Police of Several Cities Called to Work On the Case.

Police of Central Illinois have been called upon to assist in locating the assailant of Miss Goldie Hiles of Jacksonville who was burned by carbolic acid, thrown at her with the supposed attempt being made to spoil her beauty.

Her step-father, Arthur H. Harrison, has ignored blackhand letters which threatened his life and that of his stepdaughter if he did not give the writer $15,000.

Letters have been sent to him at intervals since early in March. The attack upon Miss Hiles was a climax.

Her assailant wore a long coat and kept his face muffled. Miss Hiles fired twice from a revolver she had been carrying but failed to stop him. Since the receipt of the blackhand letters, Miss Hiles had been advised by the police to carry a revolver.

The police believe the writer is some demented person who has been in love with Miss Hiles but who was ignored or unnoticed.

All suspicious persons are under surveillance and it is hoped to close in upon the guilty in a short time.

Sedalia Democrat (Sedalia, Missouri),
Wednesday, April 13, 1910

Three years after Goldie's death, Enthofen was back in the news and on his way to jail.

Jury in Clinton Finds W. J. Enthofen Guilty of Exhibiting Vile Pictures

Enthofen had for several weeks been conducting a shooting gallery in connection with which he had several Sapho machines loaded with pictures. The machines were introduced as evidence and after 91 of them had been exhibited to the jury a verdict of guilt was returned. Several witnesses were heard but the pictures were relied on by the state as the main proof.

The testimony was through, the attorneys had made their pleas and the case gone to the jury by 5 o'clock yesterday afternoon. The jury was out only one hour before the verdict of "guilty" was reached.

Decatur Herald (Decatur, Illinois), Tuesday, February 10, 1914

Note: Sapho Manufacturing Company, headquartered in Chicago, produced these coin-operated arcade machines that were one of the first large commercial floor-standing peep shows. For a penny, you could crank your way through sets of stereo cards, which, in the case of Enthofen's machine, we can conclude were rather naughty.

But back to the inn.

"We've seen a woman walking by the dining room and walking to the foyer," says Schulte, noting that the ghostly woman is the only spirit she's seen in all the years she's owned the place. "All you can see is her long, long hair. You see her walk and then no one's there."

Could that woman be Goldie Hines?

THE WILLARD CARPENTER HOUSE
EVANSVILLE, INDIANA

Billy Miller, founder of the Southern Indiana Paranormal Investigators, says they've done four overnight investigations at the Rockport Inn, discovering lots of paranormal activity, though most of it was old Harry, who seems to like a lot of attention.

But Miller and his team had much more luck at several other UGRR sites, including the Willard Carpenter house in Evansville, which now houses WNIN Channel 9. The home, completed in 1849, is considered one of the finest examples of pure Georgian architecture. Owned by Willard Carpenter, a successful businessman and abolitionist, the home was near the Ohio River and so was the first stop for many runaway slaves. The historical marker in the front lawn reads:

UNDERGROUND RAILWAY STATION
This is a site of an Underground Railway Station during the Civil War period. Runaway slaves were secretly hidden until they could be relayed to similar stations further north.

Miller, who reports about the team's investigations at millersspooks.blogspot.com, says he first investigated the building after an employee saw two women dressed in nineteenth-century clothing on the elevator. Over the course of several investigations, Miller and his team experienced a variety of paranormal activity, including "apparitions, sensed presences, erratic functioning of equipment, cold spots, cooking food smells, footsteps, disembodied voices, and object movement." There were also more violent events, as Miller records in his summary of one of their investigations.

SUMMARY:

The Southern Indiana Paranormal Investigators held a convention and overnight investigation at WNIN Channel 9 in Evansville, Indiana. Along with MESA and 18 guests, we spent the night looking for the ghost(s) of WNIN. Guests were split into three groups. Each group had two SIPI members present. Several researchers experienced phenomena that would be consistent with haunting and poltergeist activity.

METHOD:

Researchers set MESA up in the office of Suzanne Hudson-Smith. SIPI set the Vernier system up in the conference room across the hall from MESA. SIPI also set up two DVR systems and the EMF Two Camera System was setup in the main hall.

Site 1: Suzanne Hudson-Smith Office. MESA did not function as a result of erratic functioning of equipment this is not unusual for a haunt location, and no cause could be found for this.

Site 2: Conference room. The Vernier system was set up to run two 30 min. sample periods.

Ch. 1: Light sensor there was no unusual changes in the light sensor for this location.

Ch. 2: Stainless Steel Temperature Probe the temperature was a consistent 70–72 degrees during the sampling period.

Site 3: DVR system one. This DVR system was set up on the first floor in the main hall. One camera was set up going up the first floor staircase, one camera was set up to see down the basement stairs, one camera was set up in Suzanne's office, and one camera was set up in the main hall. This system did not capture anything anomalous during the investigation.

Site 4: DVR system two. The break room in the basement was used to set up the DVR system. One camera was set up to monitor the candy machine, one was set at the elevator, one was set up in the banquet room, and one was set in the furnace room on the spiral staircase. This system did not capture anything anomalous during the investigation.

Site 5: EMF Camera system. The EMF camera system was set up on first floor in the main hall back by the front door facing north. Both cameras took 22 photos. All the photos on the right camera had nothing in them but the left camera had two photos containing orbs.

EVP's: No EVP's were captured during the investigation by any of the SIPI group members. It is unknown if guests captured anything during the investigation as they have not submitted any data.

SUBJECTIVE RESULTS:

Some SIPI members experienced headaches but only on the second floor outside the control room. We also had a (RSPK) Recurrent Spontaneous Psychokinesis event occur during the convention. RSPK is the sudden movement of objects without deliberate intention in the presences or vicinity of one or more witnesses. In this case 8 people witnessed the phenomena. The object was a door stop that would be kicked out and fly across the floor when no one was by it. This occurred 8 or 9 times. In this case the "PK agent" was someone present at the convention that cannot be named, however, we know who it was. Witnesses include: Erik McCandless, Connie Boyer, Angela Angel, Dusty Russell, Ashley Dorman, Buzz Owen, Juli Velazquez, Donnie Howard, and William Miller.

During a break Dusty Russell went outside and was pushed in the lower abdomen by an unseen force. Later, in the same location, she was audibly growled at which was witnessed by Donnie Howard and Ashley Dorman. Ashley Dorman was also pushed as she was going out the side door for a break during the investigation.

SEVEN

A Room with a Ghoul

WHEN JOHN AND Linda Johnson bought the old Ritter property with the idea of turning it into an inn, they loved the prettiness of the setting with its rolling hills dotted with clusters of woodlands intersected by small clear streams and creeks and the charm of the historic home built in the 1850s. They knew there would be work to do in restoring the place; what they didn't know is that there were already residents living in the house, some who had been there since the Civil War. They would learn that later, after opening the Inn at Aberdeen in Valparaiso, a charmingly quaint nineteenth-century town in northwest Indiana.

THE INN AT ABERDEEN
VALPARAISO, INDIANA

"About a year or so after we opened this place," says John Johnson, a medical doctor based in Schererville, Indiana, "one of our guests was in her room and the door was locked. She set out her makeup and jewelry on the writing desk, went into the bathroom, and when she came out she saw that some of her items were missing and others were out of order.

The Inn at Aberdeen is a charming resort where paranormal investigators discovered a male ghost, his face scarred, dating back to the Civil War. A trap in the floor of the front closet leads down to the basement, which was a place to hide runaway slaves. Photo courtesy of John and Linda Johnson.

Thinking maybe she hadn't locked the door, she checked but it was still locked. She went back into the bathroom to get something and when she came out this time, everything was returned and in order. So she figured it must have been a ghost messing with her."

Like many older homes, there seem to be ghosts galore here.

"The house was a stop on the Underground Railroad," says Johnson, noting there's a trapdoor in the floor of the front hall closet and that Hebron, a small town not too far away, was well known as a station on the UGRR. "The Ghost Trackers found a male ghost here that was from that time. Slaves would go from here to Westville, following Route 2 or what was known as Gravel Buggy Road into Michigan."

Indeed, Michigan City, which is actually in Indiana on the state line just across from New Buffalo, Michigan (both cities are on Lake Michigan and have large sand dunes and woods perfect for hiding), was a major hub of the UGRR. Daniel Low, who settled in the area in 1835, helped runaways escape from the south to Michigan City. Once here, they hid at what became known as Low's Station until they could be placed on one of the grain boats that regularly left the harbor in Michigan City, or, if it looked as if the boats were under surveillance, taken by wagon to New Buffalo. Here the runaways would board boats leaving for Canada. An estimated 150 slaves made their way through Low's Station into Canada.

The male ghost from the UGRR has a scar on his face but he's no bother to anyone.

Neither is another ghost often spied both by employees and guests at the inn—a pretty young girl. Her favorite place to haunt is the lovely main staircase.

Johnson first learned about the little girl, whom the staff now call Angel, when an employee told him he'd seen a young child sitting on the stairs. When Johnson told him there were several young children staying at the inn right then, the employee noted this one was special, as she looked just like the one in the photo at the top of the spiral staircase. The sepia photo he was talking about is of John Ritter and his family.

Ritter first came to Porter County in 1845, accompanied by his father and mother and six siblings. Travel back then was long and tedious, and the family arrived on a horse-drawn wagon. Johnson has done quite a bit of research on the home's history and says that most of the family didn't ride in the wagon (which was probably piled high with their belongings) but traveled alongside of it—which is quite a long hike from Erie County, New York. Shortly after the family arrived, John's father died, leaving Barbara Ritter with seven children to raise.

In 1857, John headed to Leavenworth, Kansas, for an expedition with General Harney but got sidetracked by the gold rush and ended up at Pike's Peak. In 1861, he joined Company M of the 2nd Mexican Calvary under Colonel Kit Carson to fight the Indians in New Mexico, Arizona, and Texas where they battled against Comanche and Kiowa tribes in the famed Red River Valley.

On the way home from the Indian wars, after serving more than four years and being mustered out at Santa Fe, New Mexico, Ritter stopped at Fort Leonard in a bend of the Arkansas River, Kansas, to do a little buffalo hunting.

Pictorial and Biographical Record of La Porte, Porter, Lake and Starke Counties, Indiana (Goodspeed Brothers 1894)

On the hunt the party went forty-five miles from Fort Leonard and found plenty of buffalo, but were attacked by Comanche and Kiowa Indians. In the fight a minié ball struck Mr. Ritter directly under the left armpit and, hitting the breastbone, followed it around through the body and came out directly opposite the entrance.

Mr. Ritter's strong constitution was shown by the fact that he rode a mule on the retreat to the camp, four miles on the opposite side of the river. The next day and night were spent in going into camp, and here a silk handkerchief was drawn through the wound to cleanse it. After three weeks he traveled to Bloomington, Illinois, and there remained until well.

Note: minié balls were a type of muzzle-loading spin-stabilized rifle bullets named after Claude-Étienne Minié, inventor of the Minié rifle. Popular during the Civil War, the balls produced horrific injuries because of their shape, described as a conical missile made of soft lead. Designed to flatten out upon impact, minié balls shattered bones and ripped through tissue. Ritter was lucky to have survived.

After recovering, Ritter returned home and took up farming. In 1871, he married Sarah J. Hesser, and they had five children: Merritt, Hattie, William, Ollie, and Grace, who died when she was four.

Sarah passed away in 1884, and two years later Ritter got married again, this time to Lottie M. Bradley. More children followed—Jay B., Ruth Ann, Lyman, and Maurice. Another of John and Sarah's children died as well.

Kicked to Death

Will Ritter, son of ex-county Treasurer John Ritter, died yesterday of injuries received by being kicked by a horse on Friday last. He was 21 years old.

Huntington Weekly Herald (Huntington, Indiana),
Friday, May 18, 1900

Records also indicate John or Jay died prematurely, too.

But it's their daughter Grace who haunts the staircase and likes to play harmless pranks on guests, hiding items and then having them turn up, often in different places. She is also chatty, often carrying on conversations with other children.

"We had a four-year-old boy sitting on the stairs talking to someone—his grandmother was at the front desk and asked who are you talking to and he replied, 'a little girl,'" recalls Johnson.

Returning guests from another dimension also have called on the inn.

"We had an episode where it was raining heavily outside and a grandmother came in with two children, a boy about six and a girl about seven," says Johnson. "All were very simply dressed. The grandmother talked to the manager about the inn, like they'd been in the house before. He thought they were waiting for the man to park the car to come in so they get a room. They chatted for a while and then the manager had to run into the next room, just very briefly. He told them he'd be back in a minute and he was, but they were gone. There wasn't a trace of them, no water on the floor, no car out front. They couldn't have gotten out that fast but they did, they just disappeared."

Besides being featured on several television shows for these hauntings, Johnson says they've had paranormal teams in doing investigations.

"They've showed me photos of colored balls which are orbs and are supposedly energy fields surrounding ghosts," says Johnson, who has not seen a ghost, a shadow, an orb, or anything.

"But our staff has had things happen, like the fireplace has gone on and funny things have happened in the basement," he says. "Guests claim strange things have happened to them. But I'm a physician, I'm looking for proof and haven't gotten any. But that doesn't mean it's not fun."

THE HAUNTED HANNAH HOUSE
INDIANAPOLIS, INDIANA

State legislator Alexander Moore Hannah so believed in the immorality of slavery that when he built his twenty-four-room mansion on Indianapolis's south side in 1858 he used his basement as a station on the UGRR. But even the best intentions go awry, and in this case, tragically so. Late one night, when the basement was filled with runaways, an oil lantern overturned, setting the place on fire. The slaves, trapped below ground, died an awful death.

Besides the horror of what happened, Hannah was faced with the dilemma of what to do with all the bodies, as he couldn't admit their existence. So their charred remains were placed in simple coffins and buried where they had died—in the basement.

Just as their bodies remain, so do their spirits. Smells of charred flesh, screams of pain and panic, and ghostly apparitions manifest in the basement. A caretaker in charge of the mansion heard breaking glass where jars of fruit and vegetables were located near the graves.

There are other ghosts here too. The specter of a woman standing near a window on the second floor and a man with muttonchop whiskers wearing a frock coat are part of another Hannah family tragedy. Alexander's wife, Elizabeth, was pregnant, but doctors (one of whom was maybe the man in the frock coat) had to induce birth because the child was dead and decaying inside of her. Elizabeth survived but never bore another child. Because of the awfulness of it all, the second-floor bedroom was turned into a storage room and the door kept locked. But some have seen blood on the ceiling below, footsteps are heard on the stairs though they are carpeted, long taffeta dresses swish as ghostly women move through the house, chandeliers sway, pianos play on their own or refuse to play at all, and photographs in frames move to different places. The bedroom door, though locked, often swings open, allowing the smells of both rotting flesh and sickly sweet roses (most likely used to "freshen" the air) to waft through the hallway and moans to rend the air. Mumbling voices can be heard in the home, and the black-frocked figure walks up the stairs to the second floor and then disappears. Scratching sounds come from inside the servants' staircase leading to the second floor.

A visitor brought along her little girl and, hearing her talking to someone in another room, came out to investigate. The child was amicably talking to a man only she could see, someone she described as grandfather-like. Then she told them that "dad" was going back upstairs.

In other words, this place is very haunted indeed.

EIGHT

John Hunt Morgan

**THE INVASION OF INDIANA; THE DEPOT AND
RAILROAD BRIDGE AT VIENNA BURNED;
CAPTURE OF SALEM—DEPOT BURNED; PREP-
ARATIONS TO PURSUE MARAUDERS**
NEW YORK TRIBUNE

**The Battles of Corydon and Gettysburg are generally
acknowledged as the only two "battles" fought on
Northern soil, and took place only days apart.**

After crossing the Ohio River from Kentucky into Mauck-
port, Indiana, on July 8, 1863, General John Hunt Morgan and
his Raiders, some 2,400 men strong, burned the steamships
they had commandeered. Stranded on the banks of the Kentucky side of the river without a way to cross, Union General
Edward Hobson, with a cavalry force of 4,000, was unable to
continue the pursuit of Morgan, who had plundered parts of
Kentucky.

Morgan and his Raiders headed toward Corydon, the former state capital of Indiana, about fifteen miles north of Mauck-
port. Here, in these southeastern counties of Indiana, the only
battle of the Civil War in the state was about to take place.

Nineteen-year-old Helen Porter Griffin was home for the summer from finishing school when she heard the news that Morgan's Raiders had crossed the border and were heading toward her family's home.

"According to my grandma, they expected the town to be burned down like so many towns in the south were being burned," recalled Fred Griffin, Helen's grandson. He was ninety at the time he recounted the stories she had told him about the raid when he was very young and she very old. "Many were trying to leave and take things with them. My grandmother and her family put their coins and jewelry, but not their watches, in a cistern."

For people like Griffin, the Battle of Corydon, one mile south of town, is part of family lore.

"My grandmother and her mother knew the Raiders were getting close but they chose to stay along with two of her six sisters," he says. "They wanted to cook for the Harrison County Home Guard, who were defending the town."

While the women prepared food for the Home Guard, Helen's father went off to fight the Raiders.

The Battle of Corydon lasted less than an hour. The Confederate Raiders outflanked the guard and were able to march into town, stealing from the townspeople but leaving most of their homes intact.

"Old man, if you could only see our country, down south, how we have been driven from our homes and our houses burned, you might feel yourself lucky to have fallen into more generous hands than those of the Yankees," Morgan supposedly told one man as he made his way north through Indiana.

"The Home Guard didn't end up eating my grandmother's food, the Raiders did," says Griffin. "Morgan and his Raiders drank from the cistern but they never found the gold coins or the jewelry."

Heading out of Corydon, Morgan and his Raiders galloped north toward Indianapolis. For the next week, Morgan, who was known as the King of Horse Thieves, plundered such towns as Salem, Paris, and Vernon, Indiana, before being chased out of the state by a volunteer group of twenty thousand Hoosiers.

His route, now the John Hunt Morgan Heritage Trail, meanders across covered bridges, past centuries-old buildings, and circles old courthouses. Some places are now just fields, others old buildings and bridges still standing after all these years.

A Stop at Stream Cliff Farm

The road south to Commiskey crosses Graham Creek before continuing along a ridge overlooking the water. Not far down the road, Jimmy Harmon built a stately two-story house in the late 1820s, using bricks made from the land surrounding it. The home, now part of Stream Cliff Farm Herbs, Tearoom, and Winery, is just one of several historic buildings set amidst the gardens and lawns of this fifth-generation family farmstead.

Of course, a house this old must have its history, and this pretty place has the honor of having been pillaged during General John Hunt Morgan's raid back in 1863.

"Morgan crossed the creek to get here on his raid through Southern Indiana," says Betty Manning, pointing toward Graham Creek. "He found the money owner Jimmy Harmon hid in the chimney and took it with him."

When Harmon, a bachelor who had first moved here in 1821 claiming the land on a land patent granted to his father, died shortly after the raid, he left his property to Asbury College. The college in turn sold it to Manning's family, who have been careful to preserve the marks in the brick surrounding

Known as a hero to generations of Southerners, General John Hunt Morgan crossed the Ohio River into Indiana in defiance of his commander, engaged with Indiana's Home Guard in the Battle of Corydon, and then, defeating them, went on to plunder and burn wide swaths of southeastern Indiana. Photo courtesy of the Library of Congress.

the fireplace that Morgan and his men made looking for treasure.

Morgan hit the Washington County Courthouse in Salem, the hardest hit of all the towns during the raid. The courthouse, a combination of gothic and classical styles, is immense, dominating the small downtown with its nineteenth- and twentieth-century commercial buildings which are listed in the National Register of Historic Places.

Valor in Vernon; Pigs in DuPont

Turning east toward Ohio, Morgan and his men headed toward Vernon in Jennings County. It's easy to imagine that Vernon, a historic city surrounded the Muscatatuck River on three sides, looks much like it did back then. The stately old homes and 1850s brick-fronted commercial buildings flank the Jennings County Courthouse. Flowers imprinted among the bricks used to build the courthouse in 1856 were symbols welcoming runaways.

Federal-style row houses line one side of the square. Dating back to the early 1800s, they were a station on the UGRR. Fugitive slaves hid in the cellars, and some still remain.

Morgan arrived on July 11, demanding the town surrender. But that wasn't on the agenda of Colonel Hugh T. Williams, the Home Guard commander, who replied that Vernon was full of troops and so Morgan "must take it by hard fighting."

"We bluffed him," says Wanda Wright, who works as the curator the Jennings County Historical Society Museum, housed in an old stagecoach stop and inn built in 1838 just across the street from the courthouse. "He didn't even come into Vernon."

Morgan and his men moved on to DuPont, destroying railroad trestles along the way and stealing two thousand

Now the Jennings County Historical Society, this former stagecoach stop built in 1838 is also a museum. Jennings County had many stations on the Underground Railroad. Photo courtesy of Jane Simon Ammeson.

hams from Frank Mayfield's meat-packing plant, tying them to their saddles before riding on again.

As an interesting aside, Morgan had with him an expert telegraph operator, and upon entering a town, they'd take over the telegraph station, tapping out false messages to throw their pursuers off track. But when Morgan's man sent a message to Madison, the telegraph operator there recognized that the pressure on the keys was different than that of the usual operator from that town and alerted officials.

A Kindness to Widows

Turning northeast now, the Raiders rode into Versailles (here a plaque commemorates their visit as a stop on the John Hunt Morgan Trail), robbing the county treasury of $1600. But the King of Horse Thieves also had a whimsical and gallant side.

Built in 1856, the Jennings County Courthouse has distinctive flower designs carved into its brick facade. Often subtle signals such as these, or a quilt hung on a porch or laundry line with a pattern recognizable to runaways, indicated a safe stop on the Underground Railroad. Photo courtesy of Jane Simon Ammeson.

These 1820s Federal-style row houses in Vernon, Indiana, were a stop on the Underground Railroad, and ghosts from that time still remain. Photo courtesy of Jane Simon Ammeson.

Told that some of the bags of money in the treasury contained the savings of widows, he left those behind.

Even more Union soldiers were on his tail, and now Morgan had to make a decision—head down to Madison and back into Kentucky or cross into Ohio, another Union state. He made the wrong choice and galloped over the Ohio state line on July 13, 1863.

That month, in Loveland, Ohio, the Raiders derailed a train, killing fireman Cornelius Conway. The scene of this exploit is now a stop on the Little Miami Scenic Trail, Ohio Bicycle Route 3, though the marker notes that Conway's apparition remains on duty, moving through the mist, waving his lantern back and forth warning others about the dangerous curve up ahead.

Finally caught, Morgan spent time in an Ohio penitentiary before escaping. He later joined up with his commanding officer, General Braxton Bragg, who, angry with Morgan's reckless disregard of orders, never trusted him again.

In 1864, Morgan was shot by Union soldiers (or was he? We'll get to that later) in the garden of a Greenville, Tennessee, home. Newspaper articles hinted it wasn't army work that kept him busy there.

The True Story of John Morgan

The true story of General John Morgan's death will never be told until the history of his scandalous amours at Greenville, Tennessee, are written. His death, so far from a hero's martyrdom in behalf of a cause he esteemed holy, was due to his libertine instincts and the blind, unreasoning fury of an insanely jealous woman.

Had he been pure as a man as he was dauntless a soldier he would probably be alive today. This is the whole truth of the matter in a nutshell. Like General Van Dorn he could not govern the baser passions of his nature and like that accomplished but unfortunate office in gratifying those passions he lost his life. It was Don Juan and Leonidas who was killed in the Greenville garden.

Republic (Columbus, Indiana), Friday, October 19, 1883

In fact, there were several women who were thought to have been involved in Morgan's death. One was Catherine Williams, whose home he was staying in. She supposedly, out of jealousy because he became involved with a prettier, younger woman, betrayed his whereabouts to the Yankees. Sara Thompson turned him in, it was said; having spied him after crossing his picket line to get her cow, she sent a boy to Bull's Run to let the Union soldiers know he was there. She made a living after the war by giving lectures on the subject. Her reason? Her husband, J. H. Thompson, had been killed when on duty with the Union cavalry. Lucy Williams, who was married to Catherine Williams's son Joseph, also was said to have been involved with Morgan.

Many people had warned Morgan not to stay with the Williamses, including Catherine and several of his own officers. He would be at too great of a risk. But Morgan liked to brush his teeth and wash himself, sleep in a soft bed in his own room, and partake of a great dinner in an aristocratic home with doting women, and so he chose to stay.

Morgan was the only man shot in the raid on the home. Private Andrew J. Campbell, the soldier who killed him, a former Confederate man who had turned Union, testified:

> I, in a loud tone, order him to halt but instead of obeying me he started into a run. I repeated the order and at the same time brought my gun to my shoulder as to cover him, when seeing that he still disregarded me, I deliberately aimed at and shot him. He dropped in his tracks and died in a few minutes. But I did not know at that time nor had the least idea of, who it was I had shot."

After Morgan died, rumors circulated that his body was dragged through the streets of Greenville by Union soldiers before being shipped to his wife in Virginia, where he was buried. In actuality, he was laid out in his dress uniform by Catherine and Lucy Williams, and his coffin was viewed by many as it stood open in their house just steps from where he died.

But did he really die? One persistent story was he was still alive, and the body was that of another officer who had been impersonating him.

> Morgan . . . escaped to the west where he remarried and lived under the assumed name of Dr. Jack Hunt Cole. It was true that the coffin carrying Morgan's body was never opened and his body chiefly identified by Major Withers. In addition, a guard stayed with the casket throughout its entire journey.
>
> It wasn't uncommon for Morgan to change identities with his men in order to evade capture from Union soldiers. In McMinnville, Tennessee during the war, Morgan and his men were surprised by a Union detachment. Major Dick McCann quickly identified himself to the Union officer as Morgan in order to allow the general and his men to escape. The doctor, who practiced medicine in the once Confederate strongholds of Oklahoma's Indian territory, did bear a striking resemblance to Morgan. Although it was whispered about, no real claim was made to the identity until the doctor was on his deathbed in Nov. 1899. After a call was put out to his family to assemble, Dr. Cole feared he wouldn't live long enough to tell his family something he had hidden for years. He borrowed a piece of paper and scribbled something on it.
>
> With only his wife and eldest son at his side, he handed her the piece of paper and said: "This is who I really am." The name on the paper was John Hunt Morgan. While the deathbed

confession was disputed by Morgan's brother and family, enough circumstantial evidence has been produced that leads some historical officials to give the doctor's claims a second look.

His Haunted Home

More ghostly trails of Morgan's journey can be traced back to the John Hunt Morgan House on Mill Street in Lexington, Kentucky. The two-story brick Federal-style house, called Hopemont, was built in 1814 by John Wesley Hunt, a successful businessman who lived there with his wife and children, including their daughter Henrietta who would marry Calvin. When Morgan's business in Alabama failed, he, Henrietta, and their six-year-old son John Hunt Morgan moved in with her parents, and Calvin took a job with her father. The couple had a large family, ten children—six of the sons would fight for the Confederacy, and two of their daughters married Confederate soldiers. John, the eldest and known as the Thunderbolt of the South, early on demonstrated his penchant for impulsiveness and bravado when he was suspended from Transylvanian College for dueling with a fraternity brother. He took this derring-do into the Confederate army, and for the most part it served him well until the very end.

But it isn't Morgan who is among the main haunts of the house. Indeed, his ghost can be found at the Lexington Cemetery, where he was re-interned after being exhumed in 1868 from a graveyard in Virginia. Instead, it's his grandfather—John Wesley Hunt, who died of cholera in 1849 but stayed on to finish up his many projects. Thus he's often seen walking the hallways as he hurries about on business.

Bouviette James, the family's mammy, is said to be the other primary ghost in residence. James spent a major part of her life taking care of the family's children and even in death continues her duties. Still wearing the red shoes given to her by John Hunt Morgan, her apparition, often seen on the third floor where the nursery was, is present when there's a sick child in the house. She comforts them with her songs and soothing gestures. It's said that if a child succumbed to their illness, Mammy Bouviette stayed on the job, tending to her little charges even in heaven. A nursemaid, watching over one of Morgan's children who was ill, dozed off late at night only to be awakened by the sound of humming. A woman wearing a brightly colored turban and red shoes stood there, comforting the child but before the nursemaid was able to ask who she was, the woman vanished.

Sadly, the child died shortly afterwards. The nursemaid told Mrs. Morgan, the grieving mother, about the midnight visitor. That was probably Bouviette, Morgan replied, , noting that the red shoes had been given to her by John Morgan Hunt, who loved the mammy as much as if she had been his own mom. He'd bought the shoes because he had once heard her say she would love to have a pair. Upon more questioning, the nursemaid learned that the woman she saw had died a few years before.

The Wolf Man of Versailles

Probably the strangest tale to come out of John Hunt Morgan's raid is the legend of a wolf man living in what is now known as Bat Cave in Versailles State Park, near the Ripley County seat of Versailles (and you don't pronounce the name in the French way by dropping the ending "s" but instead say "Versales"). Here in the lovely woods with the spectacular covered bridge crossing Otter Creek, one of Morgan's soldiers, Silas Shimmerhorn, lived for decades after deserting his unit. He set up residence in the cave, using his rifle to hunt for food until his ammunition was all gone, and then setting traps for rabbits, birds, and other critters. He also most likely stole chickens, eggs, and produce from local farmers.

He must have spent too long in the cave, because, as his story goes, he befriended the wild wolves who lived in the woods and eventually became a pack member, earning himself the nickname of Wolf Man. Together, he and his canine buddies would go on raids, killing farmers' chickens, cows, and pigs. While the wolves could use their claws and teeth, Shimmerhorn made a bow and arrows to help in the hunt. Farmers soon learned by looking at the carcasses and bones of the animals left behind that it wasn't only dogs feasting, but that a knife had been used to cut up meat.

Setting up sentries to try to catch the pack, the farmers reported seeing a nearly naked man with long hair and beard moving with the wolves at night, the echoes of man and best howling filling the air. A foray was attempted to invade Bat Cave, but the snarling and defiant Wolf Man scared the farmers away. It wasn't until much later, when there were no longer any sightings of this half-man, half-beast, that anyone was willing to take the chance to inspect the cave. Wolf Man was gone, but the search discovered straw bedding and a rifle with S.S. engraved in its stock.

But that wasn't the end of Wolf Man. He still hunts with his pack in Versailles State Park, their howls heard late at night.

The Legend Lived On

John Hunt Morgan was exalted as a true son of the South and his mythical status grew as the years went by and the lost cause became more entrenched in the minds of some Southerners. His wife Mattie, who was two months pregnant when he died, gave birth to a girl she named Johnnie in his honor. Johnnie would marry, but she died in her early twenties without having children of her own. And so, in the end, Morgan's legacy was his romantic image of chivalry. His grave was

Though owner James Harmon tried to hide his money and valuables in the chimney when John Hunt Morgan and his Raiders came to Commiskey on July 11, 1863, he was foiled and everything was stolen. The home, now part of Spring Cliff Farm, still stands and is owned by the family, who have lived there for six generations. Photo courtesy of Jane Simon Ammeson.

Hopemont, the home where Morgan was raised, is said to be haunted by his grandfather as well as the family's mammy, who still tends to the sick children of the living. Morgan himself is said to haunt the cemetery in Lexington, Kentucky, where he is buried. Photo courtesy of the Library of Congress.

This bucolic area in Ripley County is where Wolf Man lived after deserting Morgan's Raiders. Photo courtesy of Kendal Miller.

tended by admiring women, stories were told about his exploits, and poems made up in his honor were recited by school boys in front of their class.

> I'm sent to warn the neighbors, he's only a mile behind,
> He's sweeping up the horses, every horse he can find.
> Morgan, Morgan, the raider and Morgan's terrible men,
> With Bowie knives and pistols are galloping up the glen.

NINE

The Last Trip Home

ORLISTUS POWELL, JUST 19 years old, died in Chickamauga, Georgia, having fought for the Union side in the second deadliest battle of the Civil War. Its casualties—16,170 Union and 18,454 Confederate killed, wounded, or missing—was eclipsed only by Gettysburg with 23,055 Union soldiers (3,155 killed, 14,531 wounded, 5,369 captured or missing) and 23,231 Confederate soldiers (4,708 killed, 12,693 wounded, 5,830 captured or missing). And in the hot Georgia sun after the two-day engagement was won by the Confederacy, bodies of the Union dead were hastily buried in mass graves.

Sergeant Major Orlistus Powell Killed
Winchester Journal (**Winchester, Indiana**),
October 16, 1863

He had been telegraphed to about the body of Orlistus Powell and replied that it could not be obtained
Richmond Palladium (**Richmond, Indiana**),
October 2, 1863

Orlistus's father, Simon Powell, a successful businessman and politician whose résumé included assisting in establishing the First National Bank of New Castle and serving as its vice president, had tried to get his son's body shipped home but was told "it could not be obtained." But Powell, an attorney and former teacher, who would later be appointed by President Ulysses S. Grant as supervisor of internal revenue in 1871, was undeterred. Four months later when Union soldiers retook the fields where Orlistus had died, his father headed south to Chickamauga with the goal of finding and bringing home his son's body from among the 1,657 dead.

Civil War Grief Turned into a Mission
By Darrel Radford

The story begins on July 11, 1861, when Henry Powell, son of local teacher, banker and politician Simon T. Powell, was injured in the battle of Rich Mountain. He had received a severe wound to his right ankle, breaking the bone and disabling him for life. Early Henry County historian George Hazzard said Powell was the first citizen of New Castle to suffer an injury in a Civil War battle.

Powell had dropped everything to serve his country and even after the debilitating injury, joined his father in encouraging enlistments, soliciting and forwarding supplies and caring for women and children of soldiers.

The Powells were so dedicated to serving the cause, according to Hazzard, that after Henry's injury, his younger brother Orlistus volunteered to serve in what became Company C of the 36th Indiana Infantry. He was a dedicated soldier, rising in rank to Commissary Sergeant and then Sergeant Major.

But on Sept. 20, 1863, Orlistus Powell was killed in the bloody battle of Chickamauga, Ga., a battle that produced the second-highest number of casualties, trailing only Gettysburg.

Hazzard's History of Henry County reports that Powell's remains fell into the hands of Confederate troops and he was buried on the battlefield.

"Nearly four months afterwards, his remains, identified under as curious a circumstance as ever came to the attention of the author, were recovered, brought home and re-interred Feb. 3, 1864, in South Mound Cemetery, New Castle," Hazzard wrote. "It seems that sometime before the battle, Orlistus had had his name, 'O. W. Powell' " worked on his arm in India ink.

"He was buried in a trench containing more than a dozen other bodies, thrown in promiscuously, as was the custom in both armies when burying the enemy's dead on the battlefield. When young Powell was thrown in, his arm, on which his name was worked, became extended horizontally at full length. The upper part of the next body, thrown in carelessly, fell immediately over the name.

"After the battle of Missionary Ridge, when the Federal army again occupied the old battlefield at Chickamauga, Simon T. Powell appeared on the scene to recover the body of his son, Orlistus, and in the first trench opened, in taking out the bodies, mangled and decomposed beyond recognition, it was found that the body resting on the arm of Orlistus had preserved, as clear and distinct as in life, the name 'O. W. Powell,' thus the identification was complete and his mortal remains restored to the care of the family whose sacrifice he had been to the cause."

Radford points out that Powell was able to do all this in spite of being stricken with palsy at age fourteen, which crippled him for life. According to his obituary, Powell's palsy came about from excessive swimming, though one has to wonder if he really contracted an undiagnosed case of polio, which can be transmitted through contaminated water.

THORNHAVEN MANOR
NEW CASTLE, INDIANA

In 1845, Powell, whose middle name was the wonderful sounding Titus, built Thornhaven Manor, known as the most expensive in the county and also rumored to be a stop on the Underground Railroad. The home has an underground tunnel thought to be used for escaping slaves to hide and to travel without being detected. Neither its magnificence nor Simon's success could stop an appalling series of heart-rending deaths over the years. His first wife, Elizabeth, was a widow who had eight children by her first husband, four of whom—Oliver, William, and the twins, Edwin and Calvin—died in infancy. She married Powell two years after her first husband died, and the couple had four more children. That's twelve children. So considering Elizabeth's first child was born in 1827 and Lizzie, her last child, who would only live two years, was born in 1851, and with just a two year break from her child bearing during her widowhood, she seems to have been pregnant almost nonstop for twenty years. And that's not counting any miscarriages. Whew. As an interesting aside, not only did Powell marry a widow with such a slew of children, she was also 14 years older than he was.

All this sadness was set amidst the splendid thirty-room Italianate mansion, which is now being extensively restored. Said to be haunted by a plethora of spirits, including Orlistus and young Lizzie, the manor has been featured on numerous shows including TLC's "Ghost Brothers" and the SyFy series "Ghost Adventures."

There were soon more deaths to follow, adding to the spirit count said to haunt Thornhaven.

Off for the Gold Mines

> Eight of our citizens left on Tuesday last for Pike's Peak gold
> diggings, namely: Jordan Pickering, Dr. John Darr, George
> Byer, Joseph McDowell, Samuel R. Jones, Jacob Thornburgh,
> William Lemberger, and John R. Bowers. They expect to start
> from some point in Missouri or Kansas with ox-teams, and
> will be gone about eight months. We hope their toils and sac-
> rifices may be crowned with abundant success.
>
> *New Castle Courier* (New Castle, Indiana), March 24, 1859

It was all part of the 1859–60 gold rush, and though we're
not sure how the others fared, Jacob Thornburgh, the son
of Elizabeth and stepson of Simon, died of typhoid on
August 1, 1859, in Beatrice, Nebraska, on his return home.
Ester Catherine (Kate) Powell, Simon and Elizabeth's young-
est surviving daughter, married in 1869, and died six years
later at Thornhaven.

Jerry Smith, who is leading the landscaping project of restoring the extensive gardens and is also the historian for
Thornhaven, says his research indicates Kate's death was
rather mysterious. She doesn't have an elaborate tombstone
and the only hint to her grave is a plain stone with the single name "Kate" written on it, set apart from the others in
the family plot. That could be, he hypothesizes, that her death
was self-inflicted and precluded her from being given a proper
burial.

Of course, we known what happened to Henry (his middle name was the equally wonderful Lycurgus), though he
managed to live until age seventy-two—which for this family
was a rare thing indeed—dying at home in 1914, and Orlistus,
who is buried with his siblings and some stepsiblings at South
Mound Cemetery.

And, soon to come, even more death.

Mrs. Elizabeth Powell, wife of Hon. S. F. Powell, of New Castle, died on Sunday, after a lingering and painful illness of five months, of dropsy. Age, 75 years. Mrs. Powell was one of the oldest pioneers of the county and leaves a large circle of relatives and friends to mourn her loss.

Indianapolis News, Tuesday, Oct. 11, 1881.

Elizabeth, the mother of twelve who saw so many of her children die before her, was gone, leaving only Henry and Simon at Thornhaven.

And then, just eleven years later, this.

THE COLD WATERS
Of the Upper Mill Race Brought Death
To Mrs. Amelia Powell Early This Morning.
AN UNFORTUNATE SUICIDE
Caused by Ill Health and a Failing Mind.
The Body Found Limp and Lifeless but Still Warm.

At 6:20 o'clock this morning, as J. J. Ayers, engineer at the water works pumping station, stepped out of doors for a moment, he noticed some strange looking object washing to and fro against the rack which guards the approach to the bridge. His first impression that it was a barrel vanished with a closer view, and it was disclosed that the body was that of a woman, limp and lifeless, but still warm.

Her scanty clothing and the absence of any hat indicated that she had come to the race resolved upon suicide. Mr. Ayers, with the assistance of ex-policeman John Murphy, pulled the body to shore and Coroner Busjahn and undertakers Kroeger & Strain, were at once summoned. None of the curious crowd had been able to identify the body before her brother-in-law ex-state senator A. R. Shroyer and B. F. Keesling arrived upon the scene. They had been searching for the missing woman for some time and when they heard that a body had been found in the race, it was a foregone conclusion that it was that of the person for whom they were looking.

It was Mrs. Amelia Powell, wife of Henry L. Powell of New Castle, Indiana and the only sister of Mrs. A. Shroyer of 913 North Street.

For some time, Mrs. Powell had been suffer[ing] from extreme ill health and an effect of the mind, through over-work nursing her parents which rendered her condition very grave. About two weeks ago she came here at the earnest solicitation of her sister for a visit and have been spending the time very pleasantly. It was thought that she might become entirely cured and was believed to be improving under the care of Dr. J. F. Allen. She gave no intimation of her suicidal intent. At what time she left the Shroyer residence this morning is not known as she awakened no one by her departure.

It was not until it came time to arouse her for breakfast that her absence was discovered and it was then that a note was found written by her stating that she had concluded to go away and requested them not look for her.

A telegram was sent apprising her husband of the sad occurrence and he arrived here on the Pan Handle train to escort the remains home. Beside the husband, one son, Howard, aged 20, and an aged father and mother are bereaved by her death.

Deceased's maiden name was Clift and she was also the cousin of Mrs. George O. Taylor of the Murdock hotel. She accompanied Mr. Taylor home from his recent visit to New Castle.

Logansport Reporter, Monday, December 12, 1892

Amelia was taken back home to Thornhaven as well.

Henry remarried two years later on January 10, 1894. His second wife, Emmaline (Emma) L. (Martin) Ogle, was a widow who had one son by her first marriage named Elmer Ogle.

In 1906, a really strange incident took place at Thorn-haven Manor (as if there wasn't already a bunch of strange stuff going on), and that was the murder of Reuben Bailey and the attempted murder of the rest of his family. Bailey was a tenant farmer on the Powell estate, in fact, in Powell's will dated 1901, where he leaves the majority of his estate to his second wife Melvina and his son, Henry, he requests that Reuben Bailey be retained as a tenant on the four-hundred-acre farm and another twenty acres near the cemetery. But the Bailey family were in for some bad times.

WHOLE FAMILY IS POISONED
Tragedy Enacted at New Castle Monday Morning.
One of the Family Is Dead and the Others Are Very Ill.

The people of Henry County are aroused over the presence of a poisoner through whose deadly work one person is dead and two others were made deathly sick. The police and officers of Henry County are using every endeavor to run down the guilty party and not without hope of success, for letters written prior to the crime are relied upon to bring the prisoner to justice.

That the whole family of Reuben Bailey, a prosperous and very popular farmer, residing a short distance from New Castle, was not wiped out is considered almost a miracle.

Mr. Bailey himself is dead and his wife and daughter are suffering frightful agony and are not expected to recover.

The poison was administered at breakfast Monday morning and is believed to have been put into the coffee, for only those members of the family who took coffee were affected.

There were five members of the family. When they sat down to breakfast, Mr. Bailey, his wife and daughter Melitte, after eating some meat and vegetables, each drank a cup of coffee. Within a few moments all were taken sick and all showed the same symptoms. The other two members of the family

[ate] of the same meat and vegetables but took no coffee and they escaped injury. The three who were affected were seized with a burning sickening sensation in the stomach and vitals and soon became unconscious. Dr. C. E. Vanmatre was called and stated that the symptoms were typical of those of arsenical poisoning. When the physician arrived, Mr. Bailey was beyond aid and died within a few hours. His wife and daughter remained in a critical condition for some time but they are better and it is believed they can recover . . .

For some time, Mr. Bailey has been receiving threatening letters, to which, however, he paid little attention. He was very well liked by all his neighbors and was not known to have an enemy and even after receipt of the letters did not express any apprehension that the threats contained in them would be carried out . . .

There is considerable mystery around the manner in which the poison was administered. The whole family was absent from home Sunday and it is thought the house was entered then and the poison put into the coffee although so far as known the family found no evidence on their return that the house had been entered.

The popularity of Bailey and his family was such that the neighbors have concluded to offer a reward for the poisoner and this will probably be done in a day or two when $1000 will be raised. The officers are working on the clew offered by the threatening letters.

Daily Republican, Tuesday, January 30, 1906

The Thurman Case

Melitte Bailey, a daughter of the dead man and sister-in-law of Thurman, admitted that she was in a delicate condition and that Thurman was the author of her shame.

Middleton News (Middleton, Indiana), May 4, 1906

In Jail Under Strong Guard

Did Frank Thurman assault Miss Letitia Bailey, sister of his wife and then in an attempt to rid of her, poison her father, Reuben Bailey, colored, instead?

This is the charge made by Miss Bailey in an affidavit filed Saturday and the police say it is so well supported that the grand jury will be able to return an indictment.

Miss Bailey swears that about three weeks ago Reuben Bailey and family arose as usual and ate breakfast. Three of them, Mr. Bailey, his wife and daughter, the latter being the one who has filed the charges, drank coffee for breakfast. Shortly after they were all taken violently ill and few hours later Mr. Bailey died. The other two were ill a week and finally recovered.

POISON FOUND IN COFFEE POT

Neighbors were suspicious and an examination by physicians revealed indications of arsenical poisoning and that the poison had been in the coffee. A portion of it was sent to Dr. Hurty of Indianapolis who found that it contained a large quantity of arsenic.

Then an investigation was begun and after Miss Bailey had made her affidavit that Thurman had assaulted her last August a warrant was issued for Thurman and he was arrested.

The jail is being carefully guarded by Sheriff Bell who has two riot guns within reach.

By the way, just for background color, the name of the arsenic used was sold under the brand name of "Rough on Rats," illustrated by a rat in the throes of death presumably from eating the poison sold in the box.

Wife Sues Convict Husband

A divorce filed in the circuit court recalls murder of Reuben Bailey, a well-known farmer. The suit is filed by Mrs. Betty Thurman, wife of Frank Thurman, who is served a life sentence in Michigan City prison for the murder of Bailey. Thurman married a daughter of Bailey and a short time before the crime committed a criminal assault on his wife's sister.

Fearful that the crime would become known he placed a quantity of arsenic in the coffee pot in which coffee was prepared for the morning meal. Four members of the family drank the coffee, including Thurman's victim, and although all were made very sick only Mr. Bailey died. Thurman's arrest followed when the victim told her story to the prosecutor.

Daily News Democrat (Huntington, Indiana),
Saturday, May 4, 1907

It's no wonder the Thornhaven is haunted.

Over the years, the Italianate-style manor fell in utter disrepair but is in the process of being restored by current owner Steve Miller, who in the last five years has worked hard at renovating the mansion and is also planning on recreating Thornhaven's historic gardens as well. To raise money, he hosts events, including ghost tours. Several paranormal teams have conducted investigations into the unearthly inhabitants of the house, and the Travel Channel's TV series *Ghost Adventures* did an episode titled "Thornhaven Manor," where they were able to film all sorts of ghostly goings-on.

The list of spirits here is very long. Like many regions of Indiana associated with strong abolitionist views, Henry County has a large Quaker population, and Powell was a Quaker as well. Slaves from the days when his home was a UGRR station are said to haunt both the basement of the house near where the underground tunnel, now bricked shut, is located and the nearby cemetery. Orlistus is among the haunters as well, both in the house, on the grounds, and near where he is buried. Dragging footsteps heard throughout the house most likely come from Simon, who walked using a cane, and Henry, whose right ankle was shattered by a bullet during the war and who also walked with a limp. Two-year-old Lizzie seems to like flowers and stuffed animals, and when the *Ghost Adventures* team left an REM Pod teddy bear as a kind of a ghostly kiddy bait for her, it lit up at maximum power. Ester Catherine, Amelia, and even Elizabeth, who saw two of her daughters die in the house and buried them, as well as several sons, in the cemetery, could be on hand as well.

There are screams and doors slamming. A few photos taken with a thermal imaging camera show a purple figure that looks as if it is peering in through the window, the purple denoting "extremely cold temperatures, much colder than a living human body."

NOTES FROM THE *GHOST ADVENTURES* CREW

Zak goes into the house and hears a loud knock as he heads upstairs. "Don't be afraid of me," he lets the spirits know that he intends no harm, and then hears dragging footsteps in response. He begins to feel uneasy at the top of the staircase, when suddenly he is frozen to the spot. At this moment, the X-cam in one of the upstairs rooms catches a shadow figure crossing from one side of the room to the other.

With his walkie-talkie malfunctioning, Zak has no contact with nerve center. After a few moments, he regains his mobility and heads back to nerve center. Nick goes back into the house alone and while on the staircase, in the same spot where Zak was frozen, something is thrown at him from the landing above. The audio of a small pebble-like item was caught on the camera, with Nick clearly reacting to it, however there was no visual caught. The crew seems to think this area could be some kind of paranormal portal.

Aaron joins Nick inside the house to conduct a final Spirit Box session while Billy goes through the house taking full-spectrum still photos. Nick and Aaron receive no further activity during their SB7 session, but out of the 88 photos Billy took, one stood out. A white mist, standing about two to three-feet-tall, is caught in the main area of the house. It is approximately the same size as a toddler, possibly the spirit of Lizzie Powell. No other photos from this room captured anything, making this photo harder to debunk as a lens flare or anything else.

And the team heard voices, lots of them, saying names such as "Lizzie," "Emily" (could that be a nickname for Amelia, who cast herself in the mill race, or for Emma, the name of Henry Powell's second wife, they wonder).

After their investigation, the TV guys talk to Miller, assuring him that though his house is a hotbed of paranormal activity, all the manifestations are friendly even if they're somewhat loud (the latter phrase is my own after I watched the video).

There are also orbs, streaks of light, hovering presences, and shadows moving.

Miller writes on the Thornhaven Manor Facebook page that he's working on investigating the tunnel, though that project, since most of the tunnel has been filled in, will take a while. He's been told that it is a long tunnel heading north, which he thinks is more evidence the manor was part of the UGRR. He also has a video from one of the paranormal investigations "capturing the interaction between a ghost 'passing through,' most likely UGRR and an investigator."

THE HAUNTED BRIDGES OF PARKE COUNTY

Parke County, Indiana, is known as the Covered Bridge Capital of the Midwest, an area of winding roads, meandering streams, and wooded hills. While at one time most of Indiana's creeks and rivers were dotted with covered bridges, progress meant that most disappeared, replaced by metal structures. But in this part of Indiana, much is still the same and so the wood bridges which used to transport horses and buggies now bear the weight of cars or still stand for pedestrians to cross. At least three of Parke County's bridges are haunted. A horse and buggy can be heard—but not seen—rattling the wooden supports of the Sim Smith Bridge late at night. The 245-foot scarlet double-spanned Bridgeton Bridge, which crosses cascading falls and connects to the small town of Bridgeton, where an old gristmill, still in operation, sits on the banks of the Raccoon Creek, has it owns haunting as well. It was more than a century ago when a horse, crossing the bridge, startled, and careened the buggy it was pulling into the side of the bridge, killing a young woman. She joins several other ghosts whose presences are said to haunt the bridge. The spirit of bootlegger Willie Aikens, who was found hanged, either by his own hand or someone who didn't like what he had to sell, frequents the Mecca Bridge.

> Tilghman A. Howard
> Aged 22 Ys. 11 Mo. & 10 D
> In 1861 Capt. Co. A14 Indiana
> Afterward Capt. Co. C 78 Reg. this state
> Killed in Battle
> Uniontown, KY
> Sept. 1, 1862
> Without fear, without reproach
>
> Find-A-Grave

Mecca Bridge, located about seven miles from Rockport, the county seat of Parke County, is haunted by several spirits—all of whom met untimely deaths either by accident, murder, or suicide on the bridges they haunt. Ghost hunters say they have recorded the voice of an apparition who identified himself as "Henry." Photo courtesy of Jane Simon Ammeson.

Given its tumultuous past and its ghostly lore, it's no surprise that Parke County is home to another ghost, that of Tilghman Howard, son of General Tilghman Ashurst Howard, a Rockville attorney and state representative in the 1830s who was appointed as United States chargé d'affaires to the Republic of Texas in 1844. Unfortunately, General Howard contracted yellow fever while serving down south and died, leaving his wife to raise their sons, Frank and Tilghman, without him, their two young daughters already having passed away.

Both brothers believed in the Union cause and fought in the Civil War.

Released on furlough, Frank returned to the family home on Howard Street on September 1, 1862, when the days were

Said to have more covered bridges than any other county in the United States, the tiny hamlet of Bridgeton has both a gristmill, still in operation and open year round, and a bridge that's said to be haunted. Originally known as Lockwood Mill, the grain mill was the meeting place for people in the area, and so much liquor was consumed there that it was called Sodom instead. But despite all the carousing and drunken brawling, the ghosts said to haunt the bridge are much more sedate—the young woman driving a buggy and the horse who bolted are among the spirits here. Photo courtesy of Jane Simon Ammeson.

still warm. As his bedroom was too hot for sleeping, Frank settled down for the night on a wooden bench in the front hallway. By his side was Tanner, the family dog.

It was close to the witching hour, the 3 a.m. time when ghosts are most active, that Frank was awoken by the sound of Tanner howling. He tried to comfort the trembling dog, brushing his coat and feeling the alertness of an animal when it is frightened, defensive, and on guard. Looking up, Frank saw Til standing in the open front door, moonlight streaming in behind him. Frank rose to greet his brother; suddenly Til disappeared. Frank looked out on to the porch where his brother had stood and then over the lawn. But Til was gone. Frank had been happy to see his brother, but Tanner was fearful, growling, and crouching in the hallway. The sounds of the dog's barking woke Martha Howard, who hurried downstairs.

"I thought I saw Til," Frank told his mother.

It was trick of the moonlight and the lateness of night, they decided, because Til was fighting Confederate soldiers far away in Kentucky, and so both went back to sleep—though we don't know what Tanner did.

But Til most likely had been there, standing in the moonlight. Because shortly after he came home that one last time, the family received official word of his death. Til had died about the same time Frank saw him standing in the doorway. It must have been his way of saying good-bye.

For the rest of his life, Frank maintained it was Til he had seen and not a dream. Sure, he would tell people, he could have been dreaming, but Tanner certainly wasn't.

BACK AT THE FAMILY FARM
WALLACE H. GALE
VOLO, ILLINOIS

The ghost haunting the Volo Antique and Car Mall in Volo, Illinois, is that of Wallace H. Gale, who died of typhoid in a Nashville, Tennessee, hospital while serving on Union forces. His body now is buried near what was the Gale family farmhouse, and his ornate centograph is visible from the window of the old dairy barn, now part of the antique mall.

"He was five foot, nine inches, with light hair, blue eyes, and was a teacher," says Rita Jean Moran, author of *Henry Wallace Gale: The Story of a Civil War Soldier from Volo,* who notes he was just twenty when he died.

Moran, who says she's always been interested in the mysterious and supernatural, became intrigued with Gale's story when visiting the antique store.

"I had heard of the hauntings at Volo, but I thought, oh it's just an old barn," she says.

But that was at first.

There was the aroma of burning vanilla incense or tobacco. Moran could smell it but the clerk couldn't.

"I felt 100 percent that I was being watched and wasn't alone," she recalls, noting these sensations occurred when even the store clerk was gone. "I had walked through a cold thick air going into the barn and even though I was getting all these feelings, I forced myself to go where the stained glass door is. There were two pictures of World War II sailors and I remember thinking it was sad they were for sale, that they hadn't gotten passed down in the family."

Moran took photos of the pictures and when she got home and blew them up in size, she noticed something very eerie indeed.

"I could see the silhouette of a man," she says, noting that she's put the photos up on her blog, http://volohistory.blogspot.com.

That's all it took to get her hooked on the Gale family story. Her research revealed that the Gale family were not only staunch abolitionists but also educators. Two of Wallace Gale's distant cousins established colleges, one in Illinois and the other in Wisconsin.

Ever since the Grams family bought the property in the 1950s, including the old Gale farmhouse where Wallace grew up, they've experienced many paranormal manifestations—orbs, cold spots, and sightings of the young soldier. But it isn't just the Grams who observe such goings-on. Mall visitors also report spooky manifestations—besides the image of Gale dressed in his military uniform, objects float through the air, and a young boy (maybe Gale when he was much younger?) stares at patrons from outside the fourth-floor window—that's from the outside, you understand, where there's no ladder or stairs. Other shoppers talk about a white dog that walks through a mirror, and a soldier in uniform who sits in an old rocking chair listening to the sounds coming from a music box. Just moments later, both the soldier and music box are gone, but the chair remains.

The Discovery Channel's TV series *Ghost Lab* filmed a shadowy figure inside the mall siting on a piece of furniture. Was it Wallace? Maybe so. He does indeed seem to haunt this place. But so does a young girl whose apparition has been seen as well. Spooky activities also take place at the farmhouse, where members of the Grams family now live. It was Wallace's home when he was growing up.

Moran, who continues to do research, says that a ghost has been seen in the farmhouse.

"And one time when I was there, they'd had an electrical fire and when they lifted up the floorboards they found an old backpack filled with letters written to Gale by his mother, a gun, a hat, and other items," she says.

She also discovered that Gale isn't the only Civil War soldier buried in Volo.

"Four died in the war, one came back and died shortly afterwards from wounds and four were okay," she says.

Moran, who looks beyond just the sensationalism of hauntings into the emotional core of the lives involved, wonders why Gale might have remained. But then posits, "What better place for a ghost to haunt?" than an antique store with so many familiar items from the time when he lived.

AMONG THE SHADOWS OF THE ATTIC
PETERSBURG, INDIANA

Richard Kinman,

Died March 1, 1864,

Private, Company G,

65th Regiment, Indiana Infantry,

Civil War, Plot A-814, Row 12

The only child of Jackson M. Kinman and his wife, Emmeline, Richard Kinman died the first of March, 1864, while serving in the Civil War. The Kinman family lived in Petersburg in Pike County, and Richard had the sad honor of becoming the first casualty among all the young men from Pike who went off to fight.

A wealthy merchant, Jackson Kinman had built a spacious and charming house on the corner of Ninth and Main around 1848, and it was here that the body of Richard Kinman was returned home after his death. He lay for all to see when they came to pay their respects in the west drawing room for three days, and after the funeral, on the third day of his return, Mrs. Kinman couldn't handle the thought of his being buried and so she had her son's coffin carried to the third floor designed to be a play area, ballroom, and attic and continued to sit by his side for days and days.

Obviously that couldn't go on forever, and finally Richard was buried. Shortly afterward, the house, maybe too painful a reminder now for the couple, was sold to Reuben Case and his father-in-law, James Graham. The two families, including Hattie and Sarah, the two daughters of Case and his wife, moved into the magnificent house.

The third floor was to be their playroom, but unfortunately someone else was up there as well—the shadowy figure of a man in uniform. Scared the first time they saw him, the two girls ran back down the stairs, telling their parents about the ghost. But they were reassured they were just seeing things, and when they went back to explore the attic with their parents, there was no one there at all.

But when Hattie and Sara climbed the stairs again the next day, the soldier was there and again on the next day as well. As time went by, they learned not to look in the corner where the shadow soldier stayed, and he never bothered them. But, being friendly little girls, sometimes they chattered with him, and though he never spoke, he would watch them play. Yet sometimes, they'd look up, and where he'd been standing was now empty and the soldier was gone.

The girls grew up and though they no longer played in the attic as they had when little, there were times when they felt the need to go up those stairs, and there he would be. And, they noticed, there was a pattern of what days he would be there, and they wondered if these were important dates to him—his birthday, the day he died, and whatever other private commemorations he might have had in his life—times so important that they made him return even now.

When Hattie Case married, she and her husband moved into the family house and this is where they had their children, and later where their grandchildren would come visit. In 1941, Hattie was a widow and her children all gone, and so the house was sold and was going to be torn down. But where would the soldier in the attic go, Hattie asked her children and grandchildren who knew the tale, when his home was no longer there?

Though the Kinman family had lost their son in the Civil War, Jackson Kinman, who owned a hotel in Petersburgh, wasn't a Union sympathizer, and while the county had an active UGRR and the support of many of its residents, Kinman wasn't one of them, as the following stories show.

History of Pike and Dubois Counties:
A Story of the Pike County Underground Railroad by One Who Took Part in It.

A Mr. Stevenson, in Davies County, and Benjamin Moore, at Newberry were considered friends to runaway negroes, while H. W. Kinman, Josiah Hoggatt, James W. Bass, George H. Scott and Jackson Kinman were particularly conspicuous for their efforts against runaways and made themselves very obnoxious to the conservative element.

In 1833 three runaway negroes were chased down and captured near the fair grounds. The excitement over the event was intense. The people turned out as if the negroes were wild beasts. The fugitives were taken to Kinman Hotel, where Mr. King now [1885] lives, and tied up to await their masters. The captors received $300 for their services.

Early one morning in 1852 Ira Caswell, of Warrick county, came to our house and had three negro men with him. My father put them in a heavy log building that we used for a pork house. I was sent with a letter to see Dr. John W. Posey at Petersburg, asking him if he could have some friend with a conveyance to meet Mr. Caswell on the north side of the Patoka river at Martin's ford, at ten o'clock that night, to convey the negroes to Dr. Posey's coal bank. I found the doctor and delivered the letter. Dr. Posey asked me to excuse him for a short time and went out of the office; he soon returned and told me that Mr. John Stuckey would be at Martin's ford at ten o'clock that night, giving me a letter to my father to that effect.

I went to the Kinman Hotel for dinner. In a short time, Willis Coleman came in for his dinner. He was three years older than I was but we were good friends and made arrangements to be company for each other going home. Before dinner was ready a large man rode up to the hotel and was met by Mr. Kinman as if they were old friends; behind his saddle he carried a bundle of rope and three pairs of handcuffs. When he came into the office he unbuckled a belt that had a pair of pistols and laid them on a small table. He had quite a roll of hand bills that he gave to Mr. Kinman and passed some to Coleman and me. These hand bills offered a reward of three hundred dollars for three fugitive negroes. From the descriptions I knew they were the same Negroes that were locked up in our pork house.

After dinner the slave hunter wanted to know if we would like to go to Winslow and help watch the bridge, saying that the slaves had crossed the Ohio river about south of Boonville and they would travel as near north as they could and that would bring them to Winslow. We told him that we would like to be in the frolic, but were in no condition for such service, and that our people would be uneasy about us.

William Cockrum, who narrates the following episode, which he writes about in his 1915 book, *The History of the Underground Railroad*, found Dr. Posey, and as he was telling him about the slave hunter, someone came up behind him, pulling his hat over his eyes and ears. As he struggled to get it off, he heard crashing noises, and when he could see, he saw that Coleman had knocked the two men down, both of whom had harassed Cockrum in the past.

When Cockrum finally got home, he arranged to have three African American boys, who were living with them while waiting to be sent to Liberia, ride with him and the runaways.

We got out four horses, put one of the Negro men and one of the boys behind on each of three horses, I rode the other and called the dogs for a coon hunt. In this way we went to Martin's Ford, crossed and found Mr. John Stuckey waiting for us a little distance away. He had a conveyance and loaded the negroes in and before day had them safely housed in Dr. John W. Posey's coal mine. The next night they were taken across

White River on the aqueduct at Kinderhook and turned over to a friend in Davies County, who sent them on farther north.

One of these Negro hunters at one time in Petersburg abused Thomas Hart, a peaceable man, calling him many abusive names. Hart did not want to fight him, but a stranger took it up and told the bully that he had gone too far, when the maddened brute turned on him and asked if he wanted to take it up; if so he would serve him as all Negro lovers deserved to be treated.

As quick as a flash the stranger knocked the bully flat on the pavement and gave him such a thumping that he had to keep his bed at Jack Kinman's hotel for ten days. The man who so thoroughly thrashed the slave hunter was an assistant civil engineer on the Wabash and Erie Canal.

TEN

Michigan's Haunted Underground Railroad

THE UNDERGROUND RAILROAD in Michigan followed seven well-established routes, many intersecting and all ultimately leading across Lake Huron, the Detroit River, or Lake Superior and into Canada.

Most followed old stagecoach roads which in turn often were Indian trails, established centuries earlier. The Old Territorial Road Trail, once an old stagecoach road, originally connected Chicago to Detroit, running across the southern part of the state and through Marshall, Michigan.

The Toledo to Adrian Run came in from Ohio to the south and merged with the Old Sauk Trail, a Native American trading route. The Chicago-to-Mackinaw-to-Duluth bordered the Lake Michigan shoreline and then crossed into Michigan's upper peninsula, even now a remote place of pine forests, huge rock formations, waterfalls, and copper mines, where it traced the shoreline of Lake Superior to Duluth, Minnesota. There were many stops along the way and each has its own story of bravery, daring-do, and ghosts.

Adam Crosswhite, forty-three, was the son of a white slave owner who gifted him to his half-sister. She in turn sold him

Now the Stagecoach Inn in downtown Marshall, Michigan, this is one of at least three stations on the Underground Railroad in this historic city. Photo courtesy of the Library of Congress.

to someone else. Crosswhite, who had twice before attempted to flee, determined to do so again upon learning he and his family were to be sold separately and that he might never again see his wife and two sons, Benjamin and Johnson, and that their two daughters might never see each other again.

This time, Crosswhite sought help from the Underground Railroad organizers in Madison, Indiana, just across the river from Kentucky. An active group of free blacks who lived in a section of Madison known as Georgetown joined with white abolitionist to help families like the Crosswhites make their way north. For the Crosswhites, the journey took them to Marshall, Michigan, a strong antislavery town where at least three buildings, built well before the Civil War, were stations on the Underground Railroad—the lovely Gorham mansion, a private residence, the Greek Revival–style Stagecoach Inn built in 1838, and the National House dating back to 1835.

The National House, built in 1835, was a stagecoach stop and a station on the Underground Railroad. There are secret rooms and lookout areas hidden throughout the home, and guests and staff report a variety of ghosts from different eras, including the days of the UGRR. Photo courtesy of Jane Simon Ammeson.

NATIONAL HOUSE
MARSHALL, MICHIGAN

Now a bed and breakfast, the National House was the first brick building in Calhoun County. Built as a stagecoach stop, its location—two dusty days and nights by stagecoach from Detroit—made it the perfect halfway haven for early travelers on their way to and from Chicago, another two grueling days of bad bumpy dirty roads.

But it also was more than that. Recognized by the State of Michigan as being part of the Underground Railroad, the National House, now an inn owned by Barbara Bradley, has numerous nooks and crannies where slaves could hide, as well as a few ghosts here and there.

Marshall, referred to by the keeper of the National Register of Historic Places as a "virtual textbook of 19th-Century

During renovation, a large hidden room was discovered in the basement of the National House. Abandoned bottles indicated it had been used during Prohibition, but since the building dates back twenty-five years before the Civil War and is certified as being part of the UGRR, it most likely was also used as a safe room for runaway slaves. Photo courtesy of Jane Simon Ammeson.

American architecture," is itself a gem of a city, home to one of the country's largest National Historic Landmark districts with over 850 buildings, including the fabulously ornate Honolulu House, built by a former ambassador to the Sandwich Islands who missed the tropics.

Though she didn't own the National House at the time, Bradley was there in 1976 when the building, long past its heyday and now a dilapidated apartment building, was purchased and the new owners began a restoration project.

"When they were measuring the main floor dining room and the basement room directly below it, they found a difference in size," says Bradley, who has owned the inn for three decades and describes herself as someone with a passion for history and preservation.

Excited about the prospect of finding physical proof the inn had been part of the UGRR, workers began to break through walls hoping to find hidden spaces used as hiding places for runaways.

Their discovery was a ten-foot wide room running the length of the dining room. There was what looked like the entrance to a tunnel, sealed over, on one wall. But the last use of the room wasn't by slaves. Instead, shelves lined with bottles indicated a place for revelers to party in secret during Prohibition. But that doesn't mean, says Bradley, that it hadn't been used before that for runaways.

"Because there weren't any other clues," she says, "they couldn't be positive of the room's original use."

A first floor room, now used as a telephone booth, originally was a closet with a wooden door.

"There's a trap door at the back of the closet," says Bradley. "Behind the trap door is an iron grate or grillwork that sits in the risers between the stairs. The way it's set up, someone could sit in the closet and look through the grillwork down the hall and out the glass front door across the park circle to the building used as the livery in the 1800s. But no one from the outside is able see the inside. It's the perfect place for a look out. You can imagine someone hiding slaves in the lower room and sending a lookout upstairs to see if anyone suspicious had come into town or if all was clear. If there was no immediate threat, slaves could be taken up the back stairs from the basement to the first floor and out the back door to where they'd have a wagon waiting. From there they could head to Detroit and on into Canada."

Like many old places and those once a station on the UGRR, the National House, which is a State Historical Site and is listed on the National Register of Historical Places, has its share of apparitions. Bradley says she's had only one uncomfortable experience. As for the hauntings reported by her guests, she doesn't know if they're connected to the building's days as an UGRR station.

"You have to be open to them and I'm not open," she says. "We've been written up as haunted but I call it fun-filled. I've had a couple of people tell me that there's very, very positive spiritual energy here. But I'm not looking for it. I'm just here."

Yet in one instance, Bradley was a little more open than she wanted to be.

"I was walking in the hallway and suddenly I just stopped, I don't know why or what made me do it but I just felt that I needed to stop and turn around. And there was this mirror. I could see my face in it but I didn't want to look because I was afraid of what else I might see. So I just looked down and kept walking back the way I came."

A no-nonsense woman, Bradley later returned and removed the mirror. Haunted mirror problem solved.

Her guests, though, have interacted with some of the supernatural beings present there. There was the morning when Bradley had 32 guests in her dining room.

"I was very busy, we were completely booked and everyone was eating breakfast," she recalls. Focused on her breakfast chores, Bradley at first didn't pay attention to the couple who, already having eaten and left the room, came back in. "They said they really needed to talk to me. I was totally overwhelmed but I could tell they were very concerned, so I took them to another room."

There the couple told Bradley about a seven-year-old boy who was upset because he hadn't been spoken to in years.

"They wanted me or someone on my staff to acknowledge that he was there," says Bradley. "I looked around and asked where he was and they said he's right here, sitting on the steps."

Bradley, who saw nothing but stairs, was stunned by their words and can't remember what she said back to them.

She and the staff did acknowledge the youngster and all seemed well. As for the guests, they later told her they'd had other experiences at the National House, but the child was so sad, they wanted to help.

"Over the years people step in the door and say things like the spirits in here are so fabulous and wonderful," says Bradley, whose hospitality is all inclusive, whether it's guests or ghosts. "If there are things here, they've always been positive. The inn welcomes all of them, whoever they are."

Reacting to the warm welcome they received in Marshall, the Crosswhite family decided to stay and built a cabin. They soon had another child and life seemed good, but evil was coming their way. In the 1840s, Kentucky slave owners were becoming increasingly angry and frustrated by the number of runaway slaves finding refuge in free states like Michigan and in counties like Calhoun and Cass, which is farther south and runs along the Indiana-Michigan border. Anxious to recoup their investment losses, they joined forces and in 1846 a coalition of slavers hired a man named Carpenter to locate runaways in Southern Michigan and to bring them back to Kentucky.

According to historian Diane Coon Perrine, in late fall 1846, Carpenter traveled to Marshall as well as Cass County and, pretending to be an abolitionist from Worcester, Massachusetts, visited the homes of several free blacks. He returned to Kentucky sharing what he knew about where they lived, how many people were in a household, and any other particulars that would make capturing them easier. Meeting with the coalition, a plan was formed to recapture the Crosswhite family and return them to their owner, Francis Giltner.

Also coming north in December of that year was Giltner's nephew, Lexington attorney Francis Troutman, who arrived in Marshall claiming he was a school teacher looking for a place to live.

Troutman hired local Deputy Sheriff Harvey Dixon to pose as a census taker to scout the Crosswhite family. On January 20, 1847, Troutman reappeared at Marshall with three other Kentuckians—William Franklin Ford, David Giltner, and James S. Lee—and, accompanied by Deputy Sheriff Dixon, went to the Crosswhite cabin.

On January 26, 1847, in the hours before dawn, Francis Troutman broke down Sarah and Adam Crosswhite's barricaded door to forcibly take the family into slavery. Crosswhite fired a shot to alert neighbors as four Kentuckians rushed inside and took hold of his children. Calvin Hackett, a prominent black man, was the first to arrive at the house. The Kentuckians told Sarah to leave her baby who had been born on Michigan soil. She refused.

A black neighbor, Moses Patterson, rode his horse through town, waking all with his shouts and clanging bell. Sarah would not move from her home, swearing she would rather die before standing trial. With a crowd of nearly 200 black and white citizens gathered around, Troutman was unable to take the Crosswhites by force.

Troutman threatened those in his way and demanded they give their names. A voice called out, "Charles Gorham and write it in capital letters." Next, Oliver Cromwell Comstock Jr. and Jarvis Hurd added their names. Finally, Charles T. Gorham stepped forward to say that Troutman could not take the Crosswhites because "this was a free country and these are free people."

The crowd, including Troutman, went before Justice Randall Hobart, who fined Crosswhite for firing his gun— only he was already gone, having taken the train with his family to Detroit and then on to Canada. Troutman was fined $100 for trespassing and pounding down the Crosswhite door. He ended up back in Kentucky $100 poorer and with no slaves. He later had to make the journey back to Michigan to stand trial. It's easy to surmise he wasn't a happy man about all this.

Francis Giltner later sued Charles Gorham and several other Marshall citizens in an attempt to recoup the cost of his slaves. After some legal wrangling, Gorham was left the sole defendant in the case. He was found guilty and ordered to pay the slave master $4,800, an amount equal to about $140,000 in today's money. A Detroit businessmen and antislavery sympathizer, Zachariah Chandler, paid Gorman's fine. Chandler was later elected to the United States Senate, where he gained a reputation as a staunch pro-Northern "radical Republican."

Michigan Liberty Press
July 7, 1848

> We, the people of color, citizens of Battle Creek, came together,
> Nicholes Edmonds in the chair, to form some resolutions to

contribute to defray the expenses of the law-suit at Detroit as it respects the Crosswhite family.

We pledge ourselves that we are ready and expect to be ready, to help in all such cases. Liberty or death!

NICHOLES EDMONDS, Chairman.

Battle Creek, July 5, 1818

A mob of slave hunters also tried a similar raid in Cass County but were fended off by townspeople and forced to return to Kentucky empty-handed.

Seeing violence wasn't going to work in their attempts to recapture what they believed was their rightful property, Kentucky slave owners turned to politicians, becoming part of the successful push that led to the 1850 Slave Act. Political forces in free states—Indiana, Michigan, and Ohio—mustered their might too, and fought back by electing antislavery congressmen and senators. In 1860, these states helped elect Abraham Lincoln.

As for the Crosswhites, they returned to Marshall after the Civil War. Adam died in 1878 and was buried in the city's Oakridge Cemetery. A bronze marker set in a stone boulder sits near the Crosswhite cabin, commemorating both the family and the citizens of Marshall who joined together in a blow against slavery.

LAURA HAVILAND, A DAMNED N——R STEALER: ADRIAN, MICHIGAN

Letter to Laura Haviland from Thomas Chester, son of John Chester, a slave owner and tavern keeper in Washington County, Tennessee. February 1847

By your cunning villainies you have deprived us of our just rights, of our own property . . . Thanks be to an all wise and provident God that my father has more of that sable kind of busy fellows, greasy, slick and fat; and they are not cheated to

death out of their hard earnings by villainous and infernal abolitionists . . . Who do you think would parley with a thief, a
robber of man's just rights, recognized by the glorious Constitution of our Union! Such a condescension would damn an
honest man, would put modesty to the blush. What! To engage in a contest with you? I would rather be caught with
another man's sheep on my back than to engage in such a subject, and with such an individual as old Laura Haviland, a
damned n——r stealer . . .

You can tell Elsie that since our return my father bought
her eldest daughter; that she is now his property and the
mother of a likely boy, that I call Daniel Haviland after your
pretty son . . . What do you think your portion will be at the
great Day of Judgment? I think it will be the inner temple
of hell.

Haviland, who operated an UGRR safe house in her
stately home in Adrian, had sheltered Willis and Elsie Hamilton and now wanted to help free their three children. When
she contacted Chester, who obviously wasn't a big fan, he said
he'd talk about it if she and Willis Hamilton came to the
Chesters' Tennessee plantation.

Not wanting to put Hamilton in harm's way (once he entered Tennessee he would no longer be considered a free
man), the wily Haviland had a young man she knew disguise
himself as Willis and, accompanied by her son, the three traveled to Tennessee.

During the negotiations, Chester wised up to the decep-
tion and pulled a gun on the three, threatening to murder
them. Fortunately, they were able to escape, which enraged the
Chesters even more.

Thomas Chester's response was to print and circulate
handbills throughout the South describing Haviland's work
as an abolitionist—an act tantamount to waving a red flag in

front of a bull. As an added incentive to anyone so inclined, the handbills included Haviland's address along with a reward of $3,000, about $85,000 in today's money, for anyone who kidnapped or murdered her.

No one earned the reward and Haviland went on to live until she was ninety.

Her home, which was a stop on the UGRR, has a slave hole in the basement.

"There are some beautiful historic homes on State Street in Adrian that were part of the Underground Railroad and some of them are said to be haunted," says Cathy Hoben, who grew up in Adrian, and who remembers one home in particular where a ghost from the UGRR lived.

Laura Haviland was one of many abolitionists in Lenawee County, Michigan. Her contribution to the Underground Railroad was honored in 1909 with the erection of a 14,500-pound statue made of granite from Mount Airy, North Carolina, and placed in front of the Lenawee County Historical Museum in Adrian. Haviland, a suffragist who fought for women's right to vote, also established Michigan's first school for children of all races.

SCHUCK HOTEL
SAGINAW, MICHIGAN

Though the Schuck Hotel on Hamilton Street in Saginaw wasn't built until 1868, the tunnels under the hotel leading to the Saginaw River date back further.

"I know they were used during Prohibition for transporting liquor," says Michael Perry, who bought the three-story building in Old Town Saginaw in 2004 and reopened the bar on the first floor as Perry's Schuck Bar & Nightclub. The upper two floors are currently under renovation and will become hotel rooms again.

An orb at the opening of the tunnel beneath the Schuck Hotel. Photo courtesy of Brad Mikulka.

But Brad Mikulka, leader of the SouthEast Michigan Ghost Hunters Society (SEMGHS), based in Lansing, Michigan, found ghosts dating back even further to a time when the tunnels were part of the Underground Railroad.

"I was at the entrance to the tunnels in the basement and saw three African Americans—a man and two children—standing there," says Mikulka, who made the sighting when his team was being filmed for a documentary titled *A Haunting on Hamilton Street*. "When they saw me they went back down into the tunnel out of my sight."

Calling after the disappearing spirits, Mikulka asked them what they wanted. The reply?

"Freedom."

"This was all captured on the video, even the EVP part," continues Mikulka. "I have a picture of when I first went to the tunnels—there are two orbs at the entrance."

Note for non–ghost hunters—an EVP is an electronic voice phenomena recorder where the sounds, voices, and conversation coming from ghosts trying to communicate with us are captured. Often, even though the voices aren't audible when the ghost hunters are investigating, they can be heard on an EVP.

Asked if he thinks the three UGRR ghosts ever got what they wanted, Mikulka responds, "Yeah, I think they finally found freedom."

WHITE HORSE INN
METAMORA, MICHIGAN

SEMGHS also conducted an investigation at the White Horse Inn in Metamora, where slaves were said to hide in secret tunnels that connected the inn to nearby homes and the train depot.

Ghosts from the inn's days as an UGRR station as well as several other resident spirits haunt the inn, including Lorenzo Hoard, who moved to Metamora from New York around 1850. Hoard purchased the building, which had been a stagecoach stop and a store, remodeled it, and called it Hoard House. Fifty cents back then could get you an overnight room.

Along with the creaking stairs, cold spots, lights flickering, doors slamming, and footsteps when no one is around, much of the activity seems like a trickster or two playing games—silly and harmless, if somewhat irritating, fun. Staff report eerie feelings as though someone is standing close by when no one is around. A father and his two-year-old daughter who were staying at the inn went upstairs but didn't stay very long. Though the windows were closed, the curtains were moving as if blown by a strong wind. But even spookier, as far as the father was concerned, was when his daughter gazed into what appeared to be an empty corner, and said "grandma."

Other inhabitants frequently seen include a young girl, a man dressed in a 1940s tuxedo who likes to eye the female help, a slave or two, and an elderly man. Curdling screams from male patrons and a female bartender who died decades ago trying to flee the flames of a fire in the bar are often heard as well.

One of Mikulka's team reported seeing a youngish man watching the inn's staff. No wonder workers report feeling as if someone is watching them.

Digital photos and a full-spectrum night vision video taken during a recent investigation by SEMGHS at the White Horse revealed several orbs. Photos showing what look like orbs can actually be dust or other matter floating in the air, says Mikulka.

"We're not sure what we captured on film. But we do know there's something there and we'll be returning soon to find out what it is."

ELEVEN

The Conductor and the Slave

The Story of Levi Coffin and William Bush

THE HISTORY OF the Underground Railroad is one of valor, bravery, courage, and a willingness to break the law for a greater good. Discovery meant, for those who were conducting slaves on their journey, the possibility of huge fines, loss of property, and maybe even jail time. For the slaves, the risks were even more dire—being returned to an angry and vengeful master who could beat you with impunity, sell you into an even more dismal situation, and separate you from your family and loved ones.

But that didn't stop those who were fervent believers, willing to risk it all.

Eileen Baker-Wall grew up in Fountain City, a tiny town in Central Indiana not far from the Ohio border. Just north of Richmond, the area has a large population of Quakers and Amish. For Baker-Wall, a retired assistant superintendent, the brick home on US 27 always held a vague family significance though it wasn't a subject much mentioned in her home. But in her sophomore year, one of Baker-Wall's teachers began asking her questions about her family's past and

Eileen Baker-Wall at the gravesite of her great-great-grandfather, William Bush, an escaped slave who was helped by Levi and Catharine Coffin at their Underground Railroad station in Fountain City. William Bush went on to be a conductor himself. Many of his descendants still live in Fountain City. Photo courtesy of Jane Simon Ammeson.

how they came to live in Fountain City and so she, in turn, began to ask her parents and other family members.

It was a subject that for well over a century no one in her family had discussed. Not because of a great crime or scandal but because when William Bush came to Fountain City, then known as Newport, in 1826, he did so in the dead of night, concealed most likely in a wagon. He arrived on the doorstep of Levi and Catharine Coffin, prosperous Quaker merchants who owned a store just down the street from their home.

Even by today's standards, the Federal-style Coffin house, now a National Historic Landmark, is solid and attractive, with large windows, eight rooms, six fireplaces,

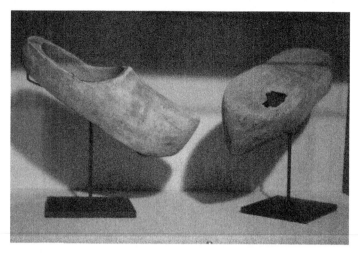

The wooden shoes William Bush was wearing when he showed up on the doorstep of the Coffin home are now on display at the Levi Coffin House & Interpretative Center. Photo courtesy of Jane Simon Ammeson.

ash- and poplar-planked floors, high ceilings, and views of the barn and the creek beyond. It was built in 1838, and back then, the home was even more spectacular—brick when most homes of the time were wood, its interior walls covered with plaster to help insulate against the cold when at the time the chinks of log cabins let the cold winds creep in, and, in the basement kitchen, a cistern constantly replenished from the spring below. That meant Catharine, or Aunt Katy, as she was called, had easy access to water inside her home at a time when almost everyone in Fountain City had to go outside, no matter the weather, to draw their drinking and cleaning water from either a well or Noble Run Creek, which runs along the perimeter of the town.

Despite being by all accounts an exceptionally good and decent man and husband, Levi Coffin most likely didn't build the indoor spring-fed well just for his wife's convenience, but

An upstairs room in the Coffin home has a small space behind the wall, its entrance easily concealed by sliding a bed in front of it. There is a wagon with a false bottom in the barn, and a cistern in the basement for drinking water. Photo courtesy of Jane Simon Ammeson.

also because the home often was filled with travelers—those who were often hungry, cold, sick, or thirsty, and whose presence was to be kept a secret.

"They didn't want people noticing how often they were drawing water," says Janice McGuire, who for forty years has worked tirelessly along with others to make sure that the Levi Coffin home is preserved. We are standing at the bottom of the stairs leading from the basement kitchen. There in the floor a brick-lined cistern is filled with what looks like pure spring water.

Next, Baker-Wall takes me up the winding and narrow back stairs, which lead to a bedroom. In the wall is a small door where travelers could hide if slave catchers came to the house. One of the beds covered with a hand-crafted quilt could easily be pulled over to hide the entrance to this tiny garret. Through the master bedroom and out into the landing of the main staircase Baker-Wall points out a doorway leading to the attic. It would be this door that hunters would open, climbing the loft like ladder steps to the low ceiling attic above. But that was a diversion. All the time, runaway slaves would instead be hidden in other parts of the house— in the garret, in-between the feather tick mattresses, or in the wagon with the concealed storage area that sits in the white barn out back.

Since retiring, Baker-Wall has volunteered to work at the Levi Coffin State Historic Site, which recently opened an interpretative center next door, in a house dating back even further than the Coffin home. But as much as all the volunteers here love this place, its history, and what it stands for, it's Baker-Wall who has the ultimate personal connection. Her great-great-grandfather was William Bush, an escaped slave from Mississippi who arrived at the Coffin home wearing wooden shoes and who was taken in by the family, protected, and helped to start a new life as a free man.

While most of the estimated two thousand slaves to have been helped over the decades by the Coffins continued on, ultimately ending up in Canada, Bush chose to stay. He was a blacksmith by trade and so opened a smithy shop. He married twice, had eleven children, and when the plague came to Fountain City, he was the one who bravely helped the sick and the dying. He picked up the bodies and buried them.

"He never got sick himself while he was doing that," says Baker-Wall as she stands next to her great-great-grandfather's tombstone in Willow Grove Cemetery in Fountain City. Bush's home remains too, about four blocks from the Coffin home, a marker in the front yard noting its significance.

William Bush, the fugitive slave from Mississippi, is now, and has been, for many years an industrious blacksmith and respectable citizen of Newport.

History of Wayne County, Indiana, from Its First Settlement to the Present by Andrew White Young, 1872.

"I didn't understand until high school about the history of our family," says Baker-Wall. "I think when slaves came here they didn't want people to know where they came from."

Bush in turn became a conductor on the UGRR, helping the many people who found their way to Fountain City. He lived a good life and died in his late nineties. His mortar and pestle, found in the attic of Ina Burden, Baker-Wall's great-aunt, is on display at the interpretative center, as are the wooden shoes he wore, with a large hole in the bottom of one.

"My great-great-grandfather was a type of veterinarian too," says Baker-Wall. "He would use that mortar and pestle to mix up potions for horses."

Raised in a Quaker family in New Garden, North Carolina, Levi Coffin learned about slavery early on.

I DATE my conversion to Abolitionism from an incident which occurred when I was about seven years old . . . Free negroes in Pennsylvania were frequently kidnapped or decoyed into these States, then hurried away to Georgia, Alabama, or Louisiana, and sold. The gangs were handcuffed and chained together, and driven by a man on horseback, who flourished a long whip, such as is used in driving cattle, and goaded the reluctant and weary when their feet lagged on the long journey. One day I was by the roadside where my father was chopping wood, when I saw such a gang approaching along the new Salisbury road. The coffle of slaves came first, chained in couples on each side of a long chain which extended between them; the driver was some distance behind, with the wagon of supplies. My father addressed the slaves pleasantly, and then asked: "Well, boys, why do they chain you?"

One of the men, whose countenance betrayed unusual intelligence and whose expression denoted the deepest sadness, replied: "They have taken us away from our wives and children, and they chain us lest we should make our escape and go back to them . . ." My father explained to me the meaning of slavery, and, as I listened, the thought arose in my mind—"How terribly we should feel if father were taken away from us."

Coffin was fifteen and attending a corn shucking when he saw a group of slaves arrive. While others ate dinner later on, Coffin went out and talked to the slaves, and he learned that one of the group, a slave named Stephen, was freeborn and had been a former indentured student to Edward Lloyd, a Philadelphia Quaker. As was too common back then, Stephen was captured and sold into slavery.

Coffin arranged with another African American whom he knew well to take Stephen to the Coffin family home the next night, where his father, also named Levi, wrote to Lloyd about his former student. Soon, Stephen was liberated.

Katy Coffin also came from a family of abolitionists. The couple married in 1824 and moved to Fountain City in 1826, where Coffin earned the title of "president" of the Underground Railroad, and their home became known as the Grand Central Station.

Some wondered why Coffin would take such risks, and to those he responded that he had "read in the Bible when I was a boy that it was right to take in the stranger, administer to those in distress and that I thought it was always safe to be right. The Bible, in bidding us to feed the hungry and clothe

the naked, said nothing about color and I should try to follow the teachings of that good book."

As for the Coffin home, escapees would knock on the door at all times of night.

"I would invite them, in a low tone," recalled Coffin, "to come in, and they would follow me into the darkened house without a word, for we knew not who might be watching and listening."

Interestingly—and much less well known—Coffin was part of the Free Produce movement, which began in Philadelphia.

"They felt it was unconscionable to sell the fruits of slave labor," says McGuire. "So the Coffins began selling free labor goods at their store here and then later moved to Cincinnati to run a warehouse selling free labor goods."

But while the Coffins and their compatriots helped about one hundred slaves each year they lived in Fountain City and said that all of those they helped made it to safety, other slaves weren't as lucky. The rigors of the journey could and did result in death for some as they traveled this mysterious road. After all, slaves swam the cold waters of the Mississippi and Ohio, fled after being beaten and whipped, wore rags as they traveled through all sorts of weather, women had vulnerable children and babies and sometimes were pregnant. They often had little food except that given to them by strangers, and they were scared and anxious of the slave hunters pursuing them and what would become of them even if they reached their destination. And the Coffins had their own pain and loss. Two of their children died young and two more in their teens. Of six children born to the couple, only two sons made it into adulthood.

Over the years, McGuire has resisted the entreaties of paranormal societies and ghost hunters who wanted to bring their equipment to the Coffin home. She doesn't want to sensationalize the place.

Still, even she sometimes feels things, particularly when only firelight and candles illuminate the house, recreating an ambience of the home from the 1840s.

"You can't be in the house," she says, "and not feel the sense of what people were feeling."

TWELVE

Restless Spirits

RUNAWAY SLAVES NEVER to complete their journey aren't the only specters from the War Between the States. Both Union and Confederate soldiers also remained behind, still haunting places where they once lived or died.

LINGERING GHOSTS IN CIRCLEVILLE

In Circleville, Ohio, Civil War soldiers have found a place to stay. Though the Circleville Memorial Hall wasn't built until 1890, its purpose, as a memorial to those who fought in the Civil War, seems to have attracted a veteran of the Union Army whose ghost is sometimes spied in the mirrors.

Built in 1845 when Ohio had one of the most active Underground Railroad networks in the United States, the Circleville Courthouse also has its own Civil War soldier apparition. He didn't come until after the building was remodeled in 1888 but now can be found walking the courthouse's upper floors.

The tale of the slave who died at the home of Samuel Moore in Circleville, Ohio, is so deeply engrained in the traditions of the Underground Railroad that a brass marker erected by the state tells of the haunting. Moore's two-story red brick home is located on the River-to-Lake Freedom Trail, which generally follows the present-day alignment of US 23 from the Ohio River at Portsmouth going north through central Ohio. North of Marion County, the trail follows SR 4 to Sandusky, on the shore of Lake Erie. The ghosts of other slaves, who, after leaving the shelter of Moore's home, either died or were killed on the trail, have also come back to seek safety there again.

HAUNTED BURIAL GROUNDS: GHOSTLY ILLINOIS AND INDIANA CEMETERIES

Now barely visible, a small family cemetery is hidden by the nearby trees. Just ten or so tombstones, some still ornate and still standing and others broken, their inscriptions barely legible, are all that is left of what was once a fine piece of property with a magnificent home. The Krome family founded the town of Maryville, Illinois, but their house was said to be haunted, the basement the place where slave auctions were held. Shackles were cemented into the wall, and though the house has burned down, ghostly sightings are common as slaves mill around the cemetery and strange lights from nowhere are seen late at night.

Known variously as Moon Creek Cemetery and Moon's Point Cemetery, this small family plot was where early pioneers Jacob Moon and his family are buried. Considered one of the most haunted cemeteries in Illinois (I am not sure how these things are rated), its premier resident is a woman who, when she was alive, frequently visited the grave of her son, who died in battle during the Civil War. Visiting his final resting spot became such an ingrained habit that, even when she passed away, her spirit continues the ritual. And because she doesn't seem to like strangers entering what she's obviously come to believe is her own personal hangout, she greets people with an angry "get out" and, to reinforce her command, carries a hatchet, thus earning her the nickname "the Hatchet Lady." As if dealing with a ghost carrying a hatchet isn't worrisome enough, Moon Creek Cemetery is rife with other paranormal activities. There's the scraping noise of sarcophagus lids as they're pushed open, bright red and white orbs floating through the air, an apparition of a young boy walking among the tombstones, and flickering lights both in and around the cemetery.

Hendricks County, Indiana, had at least three Underground Railroad stations, and the Hadley Friends Cemetery located down a long gravel drive behind the Danville Friends Church is thought to be haunted by a slave who died along the UGRR and is buried there. (At least he doesn't carry a hatchet.)

The Old Gristmill

Constructed in 1852, the Graue Mill in Oak Brook was more than just a gristmill—it also was a station on the Underground Railroad.

> In the 1800s, Wheaton, Glen Ellyn, Glendale Heights, Wayne Center, Warrenville, West Chicago, Lombard, Naperville, Downers Grove, Hinsdale, Lyons and Oak Brook had "stations" on the Underground Railroad. DuPage County was situated in such a way that "passengers" coming from the south, southwest, and western parts of the state passed through the area. Wheaton College, the Filer House (Glen Ellyn), the Peck House (Lombard), and the Blodgett Home (Downers Grove) are examples of the few remaining structures in DuPage County which provided havens for slaves seeking their freedom.

Graue Mill in Oak Brook was once part of a network of UGRR stations in this area of Illinois but now is one of only a few that remain. Photo courtesy of the Library of Congress.

> Graue Mill and Museum in Oak Brook is one of the remaining "stations." Frederick Graue, a miller by occupation, housed slaves in the basement of his gristmill. Graue Mill's location on Salt Creek, a tributary of the Des Plaines River, made it an ideal location for harboring slaves.
>
> From www.grauemill.org/underground.htm

A door opening onto York Road would have been where slaves entered the basement with its thick limestone walls. Shrubbery and bushes would have been used to hide the doorway, and there were no stairs connecting it to the first floor, making it even harder to access. The basement now contains artifacts, documents, and exhibitions on the UGRR.

Near the mill, the Evangelical Church Cemetery is said to be the final stop for several slaves traveling along the Underground Railroad, and their restless spirits still mill (excuse the pun) around this old graveyard as if they're anxious to get on with their journey.

The Tunnels of Markel Mill

The dam, parts of the foundation, and a few now sealed underground tunnels are all that's left of the Markel Mill, built in 1816 in Terre Haute. Once a stop on the UGRR, one of the tunnels is where a young runaway slave remains, still hiding from her evil slave master.

Many haunted UGRR stories involve tunnels, and it makes sense. Tunnels were not only a place under the earth to hide but could connect with other stations or hiding places along the Underground Railroad.

THIRTEEN

There Should Be Ghosts!

WHILE WRITING THIS book, I always looked behind the ghost lore, instead studying contemporary accounts to collaborate the stories of Underground Railroad sites and ghostly hauntings. So much of the history of the UGRR is difficult to substantiate because it was a secret organization. As for tales of things that go bump in the night, those too aren't necessarily provable—after all one person's flying orb is just a blob to another. But some stories have resonance, lasting through generations, and correlate with recorded history that matches the ghostly events.

And sometimes the opposite is true. Wolf Mansion, which at a glance is a perfect combination of Civil War and paranormal, seemed hard to believe even from the start. Chronologically and geographically it didn't fit, but it was such a good story that I wanted to try to track it down anyway and see if I could find any substantiation to the gruesome tale.

WOLF MANSION
VALPARAISO, INDIANA

As the story goes, Josephus Wolf, upon learning that slavery had been abolished, overreacted to the nth degree, and killed

The Anti-Slavery Friends Cemetery in Westfield, Indiana, where several Union soldiers who died fighting in the Civil War are buried, including Joseph Conklin, who perished in Atlanta. Photo courtesy of Jane Simon Ammeson.

not only all of his slaves but also his family. In some variations, he dismembered the bodies, hid them in various parts of the house, and then shot himself. Of course, with all this going on, the house should be haunted. And it sure is supposed to be—lights shine from the bell tower even though the house was abandoned, doors open and close by themselves, the bell rings in the bell tower when no one is there to pull the rope, ghostly figures stare out of the window, screams rend the air, and visitors complain of someone breathing down their neck and brushing against their hair.

Alas, as wonderfully horrifying as it sounds and as perfect as it would be for a book like this, it doesn't seem to be true.

First of all, this cupola-topped mansion at the intersection of Shrine Road and Boiling Springs Road in Union

Volunteers are working at restoring and maintaining the Anti-Slavery Friends Cemetery, which is located just blocks away from Westfield, Indiana's historic downtown. Photo courtesy of Jane Simon Ammeson.

Township, near the charming historic city of Valparaiso in Northwest Indiana, wasn't built until 1875, a decade after the end of the Civil War. And besides, Indiana was a free state, so how could Josephus have owned slaves, let alone massacre them in a fit of pique over emancipation? As for killing himself, that isn't true either.

A Farmer's Fatal Accident

This morning Josephus Wolf, one of the most prominent farmers and the wealthiest man in Porter county, met with a serious accident which will prove fatal. While on his way home a runaway team crashed into his buggy and completely demolished it, throwing him out. He is unconscious and has sustained severe internal injuries.

Indiana State Sentinel, Indianapolis, May 10, 1893

Who is Josephus Wolf? Is he a man so evil that people could easily believe such vile things about him?

Heeds Call of Gold

When the Gold Rush of '49 caused a westward movement to California, Josephus Wolf joined the gold-seekers.

After his return in 1852, Wolf married Miss Susan M. Young of Erie County, Ohio and settled in the Salt Creek area of the township. Wolf added continuously to his farm acreage before, during, and after the Civil War.

In 1875, he built the mansion that became a country showplace of the time and that survives today.

Oh, and by the way, it wasn't a bell tower but a cupola.

A tradition of the countryside is that Wolf watched the movements of his herd and other activities on his farm from the high windowed cupola of the mansion.

Josephus Wolf, another of the early settlers, came here on Twenty Mile Prairie as he wanted level prairie land. Wolf eventually owned five dairy farms

Chicago Tribune, Sunday, November 7 1965

Oh, and his family also took in other children.

Word has been received here of the death at Guthrie, Ohio, on October 9 of Mrs. Marie Wenoman, 95, former Valparaiso resident. The decedent lived for many years on Twenty Mile Prairie near Wheeler with the Josephus Wolf family by whom she was reared.

Vidette-Messenger (Valparaiso, Indiana) Monday,
October 18, 1948

And his children obviously lived long enough to have children of their own, contrary to the legend, which has him cutting their bodies into pieces.

Local Woman Is Victim of Long Illness

Mrs. Vera Sawtelle, age 50 years, wife of Edward J. Sawtelle, died at 2 a.m. today at her home in the Jefferson flats on Napoleon Street following an extended illness.

She was born in Portage township, Porter County on March 21, 1888, a daughter of Francis Wolf and Ida (Arnold) Wolf. She was a granddaughter of Josephus Wolf, one of the early pioneers in our county.

Vidette-Messenger (Valparaiso, Indiana)
Monday, October 3, 1938

The Josephus Wolf House, where body parts are said to be hidden within walls, is a Victorian Italianate mansion placed on the National Historic Register in 2007. One would think decaying limbs might be a disqualifying factor.

Home for the Holidays

The farm consisted of 4,500 acres in Portage Township, Porter County. It was the center piece of a family farm that included four additional buildings for beef and dairy animals. The three story house has 7,800 square feet. The house consists of 18 rooms with pine molding and red oak floors. The main rooms include a formal parlor, kitchen, dining room, sitting room, study and several bedrooms. The main hall includes a walnut staircase. From the second level, another stairway leads to the attic and a white cupola on the roof. The cupola is 45 feet above the ground. The cupola provided a view of the entire farm, as well as Chicago on a clear day.

The house was built of brick by 300 German bricklayers. The walls are double thick using a common bond. On the interior, the walls are covered using plaster and lath. The sills, lintels and keystones around the openings are made of Indiana limestone.

The main feature of the house is the full width front porch on the west side. There are significant feature in the molding as the ceiling mimics the eaves of the house and the rails and balusters wrap around the porch and are mimic on the house side as well. The cupola is located over the center of the house and has two windows on each side. The windows are single pane, double hung with a rope trim.

The back of the house, the west side, includes a garage, previously a carriage house and is original. The exterior is simpler than that of the house. The original doorway has been bricked shut, but is still visible by the presence of the keystone and the brick arch.

The Times, Sunday, November 12, 2011

You can still drive past the Wolf Mansion, but don't expect to hear ghastly cries or see apparitions at the windows. It's just a grand old home, one worthy of respect and admiration but not anything to be afraid of.

If some ghost stories don't turn out to be true, there are other events that should have a ghost story or two behind them, but surprisingly don't.

STEAMBOAT DISASTER

The names of the unfortunates who were scalded to death are MARTIN LONG, company K, and a discharged soldier of an Indiana regiment. Drowned—HERMAN BEBIANS, HUGH TAYLOR, AARON FIXEUS, JOHN RODERICK, AMOS ROSE, ALFRED RODER and J. McDANIELS. Severely scalded—WM. EGLEOHOFF, M. MURRAY, MORTON SHELBY, M. BRASSHEE and ISAAC TAYLOR.

Janesville Gazette, Wisconsin, August 25, 1865

The home of Elijah Anderson, a free black man, in the Georgetown district of Madison, Indiana. Anderson, a major player on the Underground Railroad, is said to have helped approximately one thousand slaves escape. He was tried on trumped-up charges and sentenced to ten years at the Kentucky State Penitentiary in Frankfort, Kentucky. Antislavery lawyers won a pardon for him, but when his daughter arrived at the prison to bring him home, he was found dead in his cell of unknown causes. Photo courtesy of Visit Madison.

Memorial Grave Near Ohio River
Civil War Reminder Unknown to Many

In a secluded cove near the banks of the Ohio River not far from Magnet, Ind., and the tiny hamlet of Rono, lies buried a little known page from the annals of Civil War history. This is the mass burial spot of 10 Civil War Union soldiers who lost their lives while enroute home at the end of the war. In 1965 during the Civil War Centennial year, 10 markers were erected honoring the valiant soldiers who were so near home when fate intervened. On the banks of the Ohio, on a sultry, humid afternoon, in August 1865, the tragic drama took place. The long war between the states had finally ended. War weary soldiers were going home at last. At demobilization centers thousands of Civil War soldiers gathered for their discharge which would end their long separation from home and loved ones. The veteran Ohio 70th Volunteer Infantry had been mustered out on Aug. 14, 1865 at Little Rock, Ark. 300 Civil War soldiers under the command of Col. Henry L. Phillips boarded the packet boat, Argosy No. 3, for the long journey to Columbus, Ohio. The Argosy 3 was not a regular Army transport or Navy gun boat, and while not a large boat, it was only a year old ... Shortly after 5 p.m. as the Argosy 3 rounded the curve in the river, called the Ox Bow Bend near Rono, a sudden storm blew up. To escape the blowing rain the soldiers gathered around and under the boilers. At that time underwater hazards were not as well marked as of today, so the pilot was unaware of the dangerous submerged rock ledge near the shore. Suddenly a gust of wind blew them shoreward, the rocks ripping the steam pipes. The ruptured pipes spewed steam in all directions, trapping the helpless soldiers in a cloud of live steam. Bedlam broke loose and 40 or 50 soldiers jumped overboard while the boat teetered on the rock ledge. When order was restored and a count made, there were eight men missing, presumably drowned, and 12 scalded. Of these, two more died bringing the total to 10 deaths at the scene. The following day by ironic coincidence the sister ship, Argosy No. 1, came by and picked up the survivors. Two of the injured men died and are buried in Cave Hill Cemetery in Louisville. During the night of the accident the steamer Morning Star passed up river, but for some reason did not pick up the shipwrecked men. It is entirely possible in the darkness that the pilot was unaware of the tragedy they had passed by. After arrival in Louisville, the soldiers were transferred to another boat, the Captain Lytle, for the remainder of the journey on Wednesday, Aug. 23.

Magnet was first called Dodson's Landing in 1820 after John Dodson who operated a wood yard for steamboats. In the

1830s Jess Martin took over the wood yard and it then became Martin's Landing. Martin's coon-dog, Rono, was a favorite of townspeople and when he died he was buried near the center of the docking area. When the post office opened on July 29, 1857, the town changed names again, becoming Rono. On February 24, 1899, the name morphed once more into Magnet and so it remains to this day.

The Daily Herald (Jasper, Indiana) Friday,
February 26, 1971

So here we have all the ingredients for a Civil War ghost story. Brave, battle-worn troops returning from serving their country in the bloodiest war of all, eager to see their loved ones and thinking they're finally safe now that the conflict is over. Close to home, the steamer is blown ashore in a terrific storm, and the boiler explodes. Ten valiant men die awful deaths and eight of them are buried in a mass grave in a small (whoever heard of Rono—a town named after a dead coon dog?) hamlet on the Ohio River, never to see their families again.

I mean, really, wouldn't that make you want to haunt the place?

SELECTED BIBLIOGRAPHY

Adams, George J. "Prospect Place: The George Willison Adams Mansion." http://www.gwacenter.org/OLDpage2.html.

Calarco, Tom, and Cynthia Vogel. "Places of the Underground Railroad: A Geographical Guide." Greenwood, 2010.

Cockrum, William. *History of the Underground Railroad*. Oakland City, IN: Press of the J. W. Cockrum Printing Co., 1915.

Coffin, Levy. *Reminiscences of Levi Coffin, the Reputed President of the Underground Railroad; Being a Brief History of the Labors of a Lifetime in Behalf of the Slave, with the Stories of Numerous Fugitives, Who Gained Their Freedom Through His Instrumentality, and Many Other Incidents*. Cincinnati: Robert Clarke & Co., 1880.

Family Search. https://familysearch.org/photos/artifacts/29855890.

Finkenbine, Ray E. "A Beacon of Liberty on the Great Lakes: Race, Slavery and the Law in Antebellum Michigan." In *The History of Michigan Law*, edited by Paul Finkelman and Martin J. Hershock. Athens: Ohio University Press, 2006.

Granato, Sherri. *Haunted America & Other Paranormal Travels*. LifeRich Publishing, 2015.

Heighway, David. "The Law in Black and White." http://www.westfield .in.gov/egov/documents/1376663863_54293.pdf.

History of Henry County, Indiana. Chicago: Interstate, 1884.

History of Pike and Dubois Counties. Chicago: Goodspeed Bros., 1885.

Lamon, Ward Hill. *Recollections of Abraham Lincoln, 1847–1865*. Edited by Dorothy Lamon Teillard. Lincoln: University of Nebraska Press, 1994.

Lucas, Marion Brunson. *A History of Blacks in Kentucky: From Slavery to Segregation, 1760–1891*. Frankfort: Kentucky Historical Society, 1992.

Mackinac State Historic Parks. "Fort Mackinac as a Civil War Prison." http://www.mackinacparks.com/fort-mackinac-as-a-civil-war -prison/.

Moran, Rita Jean. *Henry Wallace Gale: The Story of a Civil War Soldier from Volo.* CreateSpace, 2016.

Mull, Carol E. *The Underground Railroad in Michigan.* McFarland, Reprint edition, 2015.

Musgrave, Jon. *Black Kidnappings in the Wabash and Ohio Valleys of Illinois.* Hickory Hill Plantation Project, 1997.

———. *Slaves, Salt, Sex & Mr. Crenshaw.* Chicago: University of Illinois Press, 2005.

Perrine, Diane Coon. http://historybyperrine.com.

Pictorial Biographical Record of LaPorte, Porter, Lake and Starke Counties. Chicago: Goodspeed Brothers, 1894.

Radford, Darrel. "Civil War Grief Turned into a Mission." http://www.henry countyhs.org/2013/10/26/civil-war-grief-turned-into-a-mission/.

Roberts, Nancy. *Civil War Ghost Stories & Legends.* Columbia: University of South Carolina Press, 2013.

Seibert, Wilbur. *Ohio's Underground Trails.* New York: Macmillan, 1909.

Sherwood, John C. "One Flame in the Inferno." *Michigan History* 73, March/April 1989: 40–47.

Sutor, J. Hope. "History Past & Present of the City of Zanesville and Muskingum County Ohio." 1909.

———. *History of Zanesville and Muskingham Counties.* 1909.

Taylor, Troy. *Haunted Alton: History & Hauntings of the Riverbend Region.* White, 2013.

Walls, Bryan E. "The Road That Led to Somewhere." http://www .undergroundrailroadmuseum.org/.

Willis, Wanda Lou. *Haunted Hoosier Trails.* Covington, KY: Guild, 2002.

———. *More Haunted Hoosier Trails.* Covington, KY: Guild, 2004.

Young, Andrew White. *History of Wayne County, Indiana, from Its First Settlement to the Present.* Cincinnati, 1872.

Yzenbaard, John H. "The Crosswhite Case." *Michigan History*, Summer 1969: 131–143.

See also:

Daily Journal-Gazette (Mattoon, Illinois)

Decatur Weekly Republican (Decatur, Illinois)

Fort Wayne Weekly Sentinel (Fort Wayne, Indiana)

www.grauemill.org/underground.htm

Huntington Weekly Herald (Huntington, Indiana)

Illinois Times

Indiana State Sentinel, Indianapolis
Janesville Gazette, Wisconsin
Logansport Pharos-Tribune (Logansport, Indiana)
Logansport Reporter (Logansport, Indiana)
Middleton News (Middleton, Indiana)
New Castle Courier (New Castle, Indiana)
Pantagraph (Bloomington, Illinois)
Republic (Columbus, Indiana)
Vidette-Messenger (Valparaiso, Indiana)
Warsaw Union (Warsaw, Indiana)

JANE SIMON AMMESON is a freelance writer and photographer who specializes in travel, food, and personalities. A James Beard Foundation Great Lakes nominating judge and a member of the Society of American Travel Writers and Midwest Travel Writers Association, she graduated from Indiana University with a B.S. and M.S. in educational psychology. She writes frequently for the *Times of Northwest Indiana, Edible Michiana, Cleveland magazine, Long Weekends, Lakeland Boating, Heartland Boating, Travel Indiana, AAA Home & Away, Herald Palladium,* and *Bindu Media*. She is the author of *Murders That Made Headlines: Crimes of Indiana, A Jazz Age Murder in Northwest Indiana, Brown County, Indiana,* and *East Chicago*.

CPSIA information can be obtained
at www.ICGtesting.com
Printed in the USA
BVOW06s0822130917
494683BV00023B/257/P

9 780253 029829